CONTENTS

INTERNATIONALLY INSPIRED 87

POWER
VEGAN MEALS

POWER
VEGAN MEALS

HIGH-PROTEIN, PLANT-BASED RECIPES
FOR A STRONGER, HEALTHIER YOU

MAYA SOZER

author of *Easy Vegan Breakfasts & Lunches*

PAGE STREET
PUBLISHING CO.

First published in 2017 by

Page Street Publishing Co.

27 Congress Street, Suite 105

Salem, MA 01970

www.pagestreetpublishing.com

Distributed by Macmillan, sales in Canada by The Canadian Manda Group.

21 20 19 18 17   1 2 3 4 5

ISBN-13: 978-1-62414-465-3

ISBN-10: 1-62414-465-9

Library of Congress Control Number: 2017937025

Cover and book design by Page Street Publishing Co.

Photography by Maya Sozer

Printed and bound in the United States

As a member of 1% for the Planet, Page Street Publishing protects our planet by donating to nonprofits like The Trustees, which focuses on local land conservation. Learn more at onepercentfortheplanet.org.

TO MY TWO LOVES,
EMRE AND KEVIN

SWEET TREATS 127

SNACKS & BASICS 145

INTRODUCTION

A high-powered lifestyle doesn't always leave an abundance of time for nourishment. Yet an active, healthy and thriving body critically demands proper nutrition to support it. You need clean proteins to help your body repair and rebuild itself, with complex carbs and healthy fats for sustained energy throughout the day, fiber and probiotics to keep your digestive system happy and a spectrum of micronutrients for optimum health. And to fit it all into your busy schedule, you need powerful options for quick meals, in-between snacks and, yes, even desserts.

The concept for this book stems from my own journey into a fitness-oriented diet. A wholesome, plant-based diet is already effortlessly rich in health-promoting nutrients, so I felt that I was on the right track. But as I increased the volume of my exercises and shifted my focus more toward strength and muscle tone as well as health and stamina, an additional consideration on protein intake was warranted to help my body respond better to workouts and recover faster. Thus, the recipes in this book pay a large emphasis on the protein content. But rather than disregarding or restricting other nutrients, they aim to strike a healthy balance for each meal. All the recipes here are kept gluten-free and soy-free without meaning to vilify them. A protein-dense, plant-based diet tends to rely disproportionally on these two sources mainly because the existing food products make heavy use of them. So, the aim here is to introduce the whole other spectrum of powerful, protein-rich foods, both as a resource for those who are intolerant to gluten and soy, and for those who are seeking alternatives to them in order to diversify.

This book arms you with simple, uplifting recipes that will energize you and satisfy your cravings while making zero sacrifices on deliciousness. Inspiration was drawn from various world cuisines, with a mind to simplify them, to make them accessible and to enrich their nutritional balance.

The book organizes the recipes into five groups. "The Comfort Foods" and the "Internationally Inspired" chapters make up the bulk of the recipes, with a large number of energizing and filling meals that will fit various moods from light and refreshing, to warming and spicy. You will find great options for quick-fix meals for yourself, for entertaining and for the family to get together around. The "Sweet Treats" chapter may seem contradictory to the premise of the book, but it is perfectly complementary, as ignoring them doesn't make the cravings go away. We might as well make the best of it and create desserts as healthy, nutritious and delicious as possible. The "Snacks & Basics" chapter will have you make your own powerful protein bars as well as other on-the-go snacks. It will also offer some versatile basics, such as easy, protein-packed, gluten-free breads. Finally the "Probiotics" chapter dabbles in home fermenting with a few practical and mouthwatering options, including brewing your own kombucha and making kimchi.

It should be noted that two particular kitchen gadgets—namely, the food processor and (preferably high-speed) blender—make frequent appearances in these recipes. They are incredible time savers, and if you are interested in home cooking, I highly recommend that you invest in them.

I hope that you will find this book a good resource and complementary to my first cookbook, *Easy Vegan Breakfasts & Lunches*. The recipes here are created and tested as meticulously as possible, but I fully expect there might be mistakes or gaps in the instructions, despite the efforts to minimize them. Please feel free to reach out and tell me about the good and the bad, I would love to hear from you, and to the best of my abilities, help you. I am grateful that this book is in your hands and has earned a place in your attention. Thank you, and I love you.

Maya Sozer

COMFORT FOODS

A wholesome, comforting meal can change the course of the day and have a large influence on realizing the potential benefits of your hard workouts. Whether you are in the mood for a familiar favorite, a light and refreshing option or a hearty, warming meal, this chapter has you covered with an abundance of choices that appeal to various tastes. You will find burgers, pizzas, sandwiches, pastas, tacos and many other options, all developed with a good nutritional balance in mind, while paying special attention to incorporate a hefty portion of protein from a wide variety of plant choices, including legumes, vegetables, grains and seeds. Some of the recipes can be whipped up quickly on a whim. You will also find some that are more involved but still accessible. All have a consistent theme, though: They are all delicious and guilt-free.

SUNFLOWER CORN BURGER

I love it when it is a joy to get a ton of protein and fiber, especially in the form of a creative burger. This chickpea, corn and sunflower seed patty is so filling and yummy, with a great texture and consistency.

Serves 4

1 (15-oz [425-g]) can chickpeas

¾ cup (98 g) frozen corn

½ cup (30 g) chopped fresh parsley

⅓ cup (48 g) cornichon pickles

⅓ cup (39 g) gluten-free vegan bread crumbs

⅓ cup (48 g) sunflower seeds

1 clove garlic, minced

1 tbsp (15 g) olive oil

2 tsp (5 g) ground cumin

2 tsp (2 g) red pepper flakes

1 tsp (4 g) Dijon mustard

2 tbsp (30 ml) coconut oil (or other high-heat oil)

Serving Suggestions

Gluten-free burger buns

Vegan mayo

Red onion slices

Arugula

Avocado slices

Sprouts

In a food processor, combine all the ingredients, except the coconut oil, and pulse a few times to mix and break down, leaving a coarse texture. Shape the mixture into 4 burger patties and place in the fridge to chill for 30 minutes. Heat the coconut oil in a skillet over medium-high heat. Cook the patties on both sides until they develop a crust and start to brown, about 4 minutes per side. Assemble the burgers with gluten-free buns and your favorite accompaniments.

PER SERVING (4 SERVINGS): 368 Calories; 18 g Fat (42.6% calories from fat); 9 g Protein; 45 g Carbohydrate; 7 g Dietary Fiber; 0 mg Cholesterol; 524 mg Sodium

CAULIFLOWER MAC & CHEESE

Eat your veggies as the ultimate comfort food. Nice and cheesy with a spicy kick, an addictive taste and with the goodness of a whole cauliflower in there, this mac & cheese is a keeper! You may notice a somewhat crowded ingredient list, mostly consisting of various spices. This dish is still very easy to make, and if you want to entertain and wow with a killer mac & cheese, this is it. In case you were wondering, it doesn't have an overwhelming cauliflower taste at all.

Serves 4

1 medium cauliflower, cut into florets

1 carrot, chopped

3 tbsp (45 ml) olive oil, divided

6 cloves garlic

1 lb (454 g) gluten-free macaroni pasta

1 cup (235 ml) almond milk

¼ cup (60 ml) apple cider vinegar

1 tbsp (16 g) white miso

¼ cup (32 g) nutritional yeast

½ cup (70 g) raw cashews (soaked in water for at least 3 hours)

¼ tsp cayenne pepper

1 tsp (3 g) smoked paprika

½ tsp garlic powder

¼ tsp ground turmeric

½ tsp freshly ground black pepper

2 tbsp (3 g) dried mint leaf flakes

1 tsp (6 g) sea salt

1 tbsp (15 ml) coconut oil

Preheat the oven to 400°F (200°C). In an ovenproof dish (mine was 6 x 10 inches [15 x 25.5 cm]), combine the cauliflower florets, carrot, 2 tablespoons (30 ml) of the olive oil and mix. Separately, wrap the garlic cloves in aluminum foil together with the remaining tablespoon (15 ml) of olive oil. Oven-roast the vegetables and garlic for 25 to 30 minutes. In the meantime, cook the pasta according to the package directions, drain and set aside.

In a high-speed blender, combine the roasted cauliflower mixture, the roasted garlic and all the other ingredients, except the macaroni and the coconut oil. Blend until you get a very smooth mixture. For a cheesier taste, let this sauce sit at room temperature for 1 to 2 hours.

In a large pot, combine the coconut oil and cooked pasta and heat, stirring, over medium-low heat for about 2 minutes, or until the coconut oil melts and the macaroni is coated uniformly. Add the cheese sauce and heat, stirring, for about 5 more minutes.

PER SERVING (4 SERVINGS): 775 Calories; 26 g Fat (29.2% calories from fat); 29 g Protein; 113 g Carbohydrate; 15 g Dietary Fiber; 0 mg Cholesterol; 751 mg Sodium

THREESOME PROTEIN SOUP

This soup is dear to my heart because I basically raised my son with it. In my home, it has been made multiple times every week for I-don't-remember-how-many-years now. And for good reason! It offers a rich, complete and wholesome protein source in a deliciously creamy, warming and filling soup. But what also makes it such a staple is that you don't even really have to visit your fridge to make it. All you really need is a few items that are likely already in your pantry.

Serves 3

⅓ cup (58 g) uncooked quinoa

⅓ cup (133 g) dried green lentils

⅓ cup (63 g) uncooked brown rice

5 cups (1.2 L) vegetable stock or water, divided

1 bay leaf

1 tsp (1 g) dried thyme

Salt

¾ cup (105 g) raw cashews

Freshly ground black pepper

Topping Suggestions

2 tbsp (30 ml) coconut oil

⅓ cup (45 g) pine nuts

⅓ cup (32 g) chopped fresh mint leaves

Rinse the quinoa, lentils and rice. In a large pot, bring 4 cups (946 ml) of the vegetable stock (or water) to a boil and add the rinsed grains. Add the bay leaf, thyme and salt to taste, lower the heat and let simmer for about 25 minutes. In the meantime, in a high-speed blender, combine the cashews, remaining cup (235 ml) of vegetable stock and the pepper, and blend until smooth. Add the cashew mixture to the soup, stir and let simmer for another 5 minutes.

To prepare the topping, heat the coconut oil in a medium skillet over medium heat. Add the pine nuts, stir and toast until they turn golden brown, about 5 minutes. Serve the soup in bowls, topped with the toasted pine nuts and mint leaves.

PER SERVING (3 SERVINGS): 433 Calories; 19 g Fat (39.0% calories from fat); 17 g Protein; 52 g Carbohydrate; 9 g Dietary Fiber; 0 mg Cholesterol; 12 mg Sodium

SPAGHETTI WITH BLACK BEAN WALNUT VEGBALLS

Without a doubt, if you want to feel full, all fueled up and comforted, you really can't go wrong with spaghetti and vegballs, served with a rich but easy homemade marinara sauce. It makes for a great lunch option, or the dinner choice after an active day. The vegballs, cooked or uncooked, can be stored in the freezer as a terrific protein option, perhaps to be enjoyed in a salad or sandwich.

Serves 4

Spaghetti

1 (1-lb [455-g]) package gluten-free spaghetti

Vegballs

½ red onion

2 cloves garlic

½ cup (30 g) chopped fresh parsley

1 (15-oz [425-g]) can black beans, drained and rinsed

1 cup (128 g) cooked brown rice

1 cup (70 g) packed chopped portobello mushrooms

1 tsp (1 g) dried thyme

1 tsp (2 g) dried oregano

1 tsp (3 g) ground cumin

Salt and freshly ground black pepper

½ cup (60 g) gluten-free vegan bread crumbs

½ cup (55 g) walnut pieces

Olive oil for panfrying

Marinara Sauce

1 tbsp (15 ml) olive oil

1 bay leaf

1 (15-oz [425-g]) can tomato sauce

1 tbsp (16 g) tomato paste

1 tsp (1 g) dried thyme

1 tsp (2 g) dried oregano

¼ tsp freshly ground black pepper

Salt

Cook the spaghetti according to the package directions.

Meanwhile, make the vegballs. Coarsely chop the onion, garlic and parsley and place them in a food processor. Add the black beans, cooked rice, mushrooms, herbs, cumin, salt and pepper. Pulse until the mixture attains a moderately chunky texture. Add the bread crumbs and walnuts and stir to combine. Shape the mixture into 2-inch (5-cm)-diameter vegballs; you may want to flatten them a little bit for easier cooking.

Pour enough olive oil into a skillet to form a thin layer on the bottom and heat over medium heat. Cook the vegballs for about 5 minutes on each side, or until they get a golden brown crust.

To make the marinara sauce, heat the olive oil in a saucepan over medium-low heat. Add the rest of the marinara sauce ingredients, bring to a simmer and let cook for 10 minutes. Adjust the consistency to your liking by adding water as needed, 1 tablespoon (15 ml) at a time.

Serve the vegballs over the spaghetti along with a generous helping of the sauce.

PER SERVING (4 SERVINGS): 777 Calories; 19 g Fat (20.8% calories from fat); 26 g Protein; 137 g Carbohydrate; 13 g Dietary Fiber; 0 mg Cholesterol; 1139 mg Sodium

GARBANZO BEAN FLOUR OMELETS

This was one of the best vegan replacements for egg omelets I have tried so far. Similar in texture, taste and feel but much richer and cleaner, it makes for a delicious and nutritious breakfast with all of the protein and none of the cholesterol.

Serves 4

Omelet Batter

1 cup (125 g) garbanzo bean flour

½ tsp garlic powder

½ tsp onion powder

¼ tsp freshly ground black pepper

2 tbsp (16 g) nutritional yeast

½ tsp baking soda

¼ tsp salt

1 tsp (5 ml) apple cider vinegar

To Cook and Serve

1 tbsp (15 ml) coconut oil or olive oil, divided

1 avocado, peeled, pitted and sliced

Handful of mixed greens

4 cherry tomatoes, chopped or sliced

Red pepper flakes

In a bowl, thoroughly stir together the omelet batter ingredients with 1 cup (235 ml) of water. Heat ¾ teaspoon of the coconut oil in a skillet over medium-high heat. Pour one-quarter of the omelet batter into the pan and cook each side until it turns golden brown, about 3 minutes per side. Repeat three times to cook the rest of the batter. Serve with avocado, greens, tomatoes and red pepper flakes.

PER SERVING (4 SERVINGS): 227 Calories; 13 g Fat (50.1% calories from fat); 9 g Protein; 21 g Carbohydrate; 6 g Dietary Fiber; 0 mg Cholesterol; 317 mg Sodium

CHICKPEA TOFU WITH TAHINI SAUCE

The nice thing about tofu is that it is protein dense and can easily be incorporated into a dish to improve the protein stats. In a similar fashion, these richly seasoned and flavorful chickpea-based protein powerhouses are great for topping salads or other dishes. Unlike tofu, they are more like firm bread in consistency, quite fun and filling.

Serves 4

Chickpea Tofu

2 cups (250 g) garbanzo bean flour

¼ cup (43 g) nutritional yeast

2 tsp (5 g) ground cumin

½ tsp garlic powder

1 tsp (2 g) freshly ground black pepper

¼ tsp cayenne pepper

1 tbsp (15 ml) coconut oil or olive oil

1½ tsp (9 g) salt

Tahini Sauce

¼ cup (60 g) tahini

1 clove garlic, minced

1 tsp (5 ml) apple cider vinegar

Freshly ground black pepper

1 tbsp (8 g) black sesame seeds (optional)

To Serve

2 cups (40 g) arugula

Preheat the oven to 400°F (200°C). In a large bowl, combine all the chickpea tofu ingredients with ¾ cup (175 ml) of water and mix well. Line a baking pan (I used a 5 x 7–inch [12.5 x 18–cm] pan) with parchment paper, and pour in the batter. Bake for 20 minutes, or until a toothpick inserted into the center comes out clean. Remove from the oven, let cool completely and cut into bite-size pieces.

In a separate bowl, mix together the tahini sauce ingredients and 2 tablespoons (30 ml) of water (add more water if the tahini is too thick). Serve the chickpea tofu on a bed of arugula, topped with the tahini sauce.

PER SERVING (4 SERVINGS): 359 Calories; 17 g Fat (40.4% calories from fat); 19 g Protein; 37 g Carbohydrate; 10 g Dietary Fiber; 0 mg Cholesterol; 859 mg Sodium

TWICE-BAKED POTATOES

Baked potatoes are blended with chickpeas, among other ingredients, that turn them into a creamy and delicious powerhouse, with energizing wholesome carbs along with the protein and fiber from chickpeas. The second round of baking develops the flavors further to achieve the magical status. I know I will be making this again and again.

Serves 4

4 russet potatoes

1 (15-oz [425-g]) can chickpeas, drained and rinsed

1 (14-oz [397-g]) can coconut cream or milk

½ cup (60 g) shredded vegan cheddar or mozzarella cheese

3 tbsp (23 g) chopped pickled jalapeño pepper

1 tsp (3 g) ground cumin

½ tsp dried thyme

1 tsp (3 g) garlic powder

1 tsp (2 g) onion powder

Salt and freshly ground black pepper

Optional Toppings

Smoked paprika

Chopped fresh parsley

Preheat the oven to 400°F (200°C). Wash the potatoes and poke them a few times with a fork. Bake for 1 hour, or until tender. Remove from the oven and lower the oven temperature to 350°F (175°C). Cut the potatoes in half lengthwise and scoop the insides into a food processor. Don't scoop all the way, though; the potato shells should still be able to retain their shape. Add the remaining ingredients, except the toppings, to the food processor and process until smooth. Stuff the filling back into the potato shells, sprinkle with smoked paprika and bake at 350°F (175°C) for another 20 minutes. Top with chopped parsley before serving.

PER SERVING (4 SERVINGS): 839 Calories; 44 g Fat (45.7% calories from fat); 27 g Protein; 92 g Carbohydrate; 22 g Dietary Fiber; 0 mg Cholesterol; 283 mg Sodium

CREAM OF MUSHROOM SPAGHETTI WITH HEMP SEEDS

As quick and easy as it is tasty and wholesome, this dish will have mushroom lovers develop a certain attachment to its umami goodness. The taste aside, various gluten-free pasta options, whether legume-, rice- or quinoa-based, come with a considerable amount of protein. To add an extra kick and diversify the protein content, this recipe incorporates hemp seeds that are also a welcome addition to the texture.

Serves 4

1 lb (454 g) gluten-free spaghetti

2 tbsp (30 ml) coconut oil or olive oil

½ onion, chopped

2 cloves garlic, minced

½ jalapeño pepper, seeded and finely chopped

8 oz (227 g) mushrooms, sliced (I used cremini)

1 tsp (3 g) grated fresh ginger

½ cup (120 ml) coconut cream or coconut milk

1 tbsp (15 ml) freshly squeezed lime juice

Salt and freshly ground black pepper

¼ cup (45 g) hemp seeds

Cook the spaghetti according to the package directions. Heat the coconut oil in a large skillet over medium heat, add the onion, garlic and jalapeño and cook for 5 minutes. Add the mushrooms and cook for another 8 minutes. Add the ginger, coconut cream, lime juice and salt and pepper to taste and cook for 2 more minutes. Pour the mushroom cream sauce over the spaghetti, sprinkle with the hemp seeds and serve.

PER SERVING (4 SERVINGS): 629 Calories; 26 g Fat (34.9% calories from fat); 16 g Protein; 93 g Carbohydrate; 4 g Dietary Fiber; 0 mg Cholesterol; 14 mg Sodium

BUFFALO CAULIFLOWER

Enjoy this favorite treat and party snack in its healthy and nourishing form. Cauliflower is coated in a spicy and rich buffalo sauce that incorporates garbanzo bean flour for a kick of protein, alongside a sunflower seed–based ranch sauce.

Serves 3 to 4

Sunflower Ranch Sauce

½ cup (73 g) raw sunflower seeds

2 tbsp (30 ml) apple cider vinegar

⅓ cup (80 ml) plant-based milk

2 tbsp (30 ml) olive oil

½ tsp salt

1 tsp (2 g) onion powder

½ tsp garlic powder

1 tsp (5 ml) pure maple syrup or agave nectar

1 tsp (1 g) dried dill

1 tsp (2 g) dried oregano

1 tsp (1 g) dried thyme

Buffalo Cauliflower

½ cup (63 g) garbanzo bean flour

2 tbsp (30 ml) olive oil, plus more for pan (optional)

1½ tsp (5 g) garlic powder

½ tsp salt

¼ tsp freshly ground black pepper

¼ tsp smoked paprika

¼ tsp dried thyme

⅓ cup (80 ml) hot sauce

1 medium head cauliflower, cut into florets

Coconut oil, for baking sheet

Preheat the oven to 400°F (200°C). In a blender, combine all the sunflower ranch sauce ingredients with ½ cup (120 ml) of water, blend until smooth and set aside. In a large bowl, stir together all the buffalo cauliflower ingredients, except the cauliflower, and ½ cup (120 ml) of water. Add the cauliflower florets and mix until they are uniformly coated with the buffalo batter. Transfer the cauliflower to a piece of parchment paper or a baking sheet lightly coated with oil. Bake for 25 minutes and serve hot with the sunflower ranch sauce on the side.

> **PER SERVING (4 SERVINGS):** 296 Calories; 24 g Fat (68.8% calories from fat); 8 g Protein; 16 g Carbohydrate; 5 g Dietary Fiber; 0 mg Cholesterol; 1050 mg Sodium

GREEN LENTIL SHEPHERD'S PIE

I can't say enough good things about the much underappreciated delicious powerhouses that are lentils. They are one of the densest plant-based protein sources out there, not to mention their high soluble fiber content. With the earthy, meaty flavor of green lentils and their firm, chewy texture, this dish is filling, warming, comforting and nourishing on so many levels.

Serves 4

8 medium potatoes

⅓ cup (80 ml) plant-based milk, warmed

¼ cup (55 g) vegan butter

Salt and freshly ground black pepper

3 tbsp (45 ml) coconut oil or olive oil, divided

2 large portobello mushrooms, sliced

1 medium onion, chopped

1 clove garlic, chopped

1 tsp (3 g) grated fresh ginger

1 carrot, chopped

1 stalk celery, chopped

1 (15-oz [425-g]) can tomato sauce

1 tbsp (16 g) tomato paste

1 cup (235 ml) vegetable stock or water

1 tbsp (15 ml) coconut aminos (optional)

1 tsp (5 ml) hot sauce

2 tbsp (16 g) arrowroot starch or cornstarch

1½ cups (297 g) cooked green lentils (preferably French green lentils)

Place the potatoes in a large pot, cover with water, add salt and bring to a boil. Let boil until the potatoes are soft (poke with a fork to test). When they are done, peel and mash the potatoes with a fork. While the potatoes are still hot, add the warm milk, butter and salt and pepper to taste, mix well and set aside. Heat 1 tablespoon (15 ml) of the coconut oil in a skillet over medium-high heat, add the mushrooms and sauté for 5 minutes. Preheat the oven to 400°F (200°C).

Meanwhile, heat the remaining 2 tablespoons (30 ml) of coconut oil in a large cast-iron skillet or Dutch oven over medium-high heat. Add the onion and cook for 5 minutes. Add the garlic, ginger, carrot and celery, stir and cook for 2 minutes. Add the tomato sauce, tomato paste, vegetable stock, coconut aminos (if using) and hot sauce, lower the heat to medium and cook for 15 minutes. Add the arrowroot starch, stir to combine and add the lentils. Cook for 5 more minutes, turn off the heat and add the mushrooms. Cover the top of the filling with the mashed potatoes, and place the pan in the oven to bake for 15 minutes.

PER SERVING (4 SERVINGS): 603 Calories; 23 g Fat (32.3% calories from fat); 19 g Protein; 89 g Carbohydrate; 16 g Dietary Fiber; 1 mg Cholesterol; 1280 mg Sodium

MUSHROOM LASAGNE

Look no further when you need to please, fill and nourish a crowd. This is seriously delicious, as attested by the disappearance of the whole tray before it has a chance to get cold, every time I make it.

Serves 4

Mushroom Filling

2 tbsp (30 ml) olive oil

1 red onion, chopped

2 cloves garlic, minced

½ tsp red pepper flakes

Salt and freshly ground black pepper

8 oz (240 g) portobello or button mushrooms

½ cup (86 g) cooked black beans

1½ cups (180 g) shredded vegan mozzarella cheese

Lasagne

26 oz (737 g) marinara sauce

9 oz (255 g) gluten-free lasagna noodles

½ cup (20 g) tightly packed fresh basil

½ cup (60 g) shredded vegan mozzarella cheese

Preheat the oven to 350°F (175°C). Heat the olive oil in a large sauté pan, add the onion and garlic and cook for a minute. Add the red pepper flakes and salt and black pepper to taste and cook for 3 minutes. Add the mushrooms, cook for another 5 minutes and let cool. Transfer the mushroom mixture to a food processor, add the black beans and cheese and pulse a few times to break down and combine, but leave a coarse texture.

Start assembling the lasagne by spreading a layer of the marinara sauce on the bottom of a baking dish (mine was 9 x 13 inches [23 x 33 cm]). Add two layers of uncooked lasagne noodles with a layer of marinara sauce (no basil) in between. Add half of the mushroom mix along with half of the basil leaves. Add two more layers of noodles with marinara sauce in between. Spread the rest of the mushroom mix and the basil leaves. Finally, add two more layers of noodles with marinara sauce in between. Spread marinara sauce on top of the assembled lasagne and sprinkle with the mozzarella. Cover the dish with foil and bake for 45 minutes.

PER SERVING (4 SERVINGS): 794 Calories; 23 g Fat (29.2% calories from fat); 13 g Protein; 115 g Carbohydrate; 11 g Dietary Fiber; 0 mg Cholesterol; 1328 mg Sodium

PARMESAN SPAGHETTI

Using a trusty and simple plant-based Parmesan, this spaghetti is irresistibly cheesy, lending a wonderful flavor to the chickpeas while complementing their protein content with cashews.

Serves 3

8 oz (227 g) gluten-free spaghetti

1½ cups (355 ml) plant-based milk

2 tbsp (16 g) arrowroot starch

Parmesan

¾ cup (105 g) raw cashews

3 tbsp (24 g) nutritional yeast

⅛ tsp garlic powder

¼ tsp salt

Chickpeas

2 tbsp (30 ml) olive oil

2 cloves garlic, minced

¼ cup (32 g) nutritional yeast

Salt and freshly ground black pepper

1 (15-oz [425-g]) can chickpeas, drained and rinsed

Serving Suggestions

¼ cup (30 g) pickled jalapeño peppers, drained

Hemp seeds

Red pepper flakes

Chopped parsley

Cook the spaghetti according to the package directions and set aside. Combine the milk with the arrowroot starch, mix well and set aside. In a food processor, combine all the Parmesan ingredients, process and set aside.

To cook the chickpeas, heat the olive oil in a skillet over medium heat. Add the garlic and cook for 1 minute. Add the milk mixture and stir well. Add ½ cup (65 g) of the Parmesan mixture, the nutritional yeast and salt and black pepper to taste, stir and cook for 1 minute. Add the chickpeas and keep stirring for 1 to 2 minutes, or until the sauce starts to thicken. Finally, add the cooked, drained spaghetti and toss until it is uniformly coated. Serve the pasta sprinkled with the rest of the Parmesan, and (if using) with pickled jalapeños, hemp seeds, red pepper flakes and chopped parsley.

PER SERVING (3 SERVINGS): 869 Calories; 34 g Fat (33.5% calories from fat); 33 g Protein; 121 g Carbohydrate; 16 g Dietary Fiber; 0 mg Cholesterol; 627 mg Sodium

POTATO LENTIL CAKES

Golden brown potato patties, when bitten into, reveal a delicious and textural mix of mushroom and lentils, and they are as pleasing to the eye as they are to the taste buds. With a good amount of wholesome carbs, and the protein duo of potatoes and lentils, these are ready to fuel you for any meal of the day, and as on-the-go bites.

Serves 3

10 medium gold potatoes

1 bay leaf

Salt

1 cup (128 g) potato starch, plus more for dusting

Stuffing

2 tbsp (30 ml) olive oil

1 medium onion, chopped

4 oz (113 g) shiitake mushrooms (or other kind)

¾ cup (150 g) dried green lentils (preferably French lentils), cooked

Salt and freshly ground black pepper

Coconut oil for panfrying

In a large pot, combine the potatoes, the bay leaf, some salt and 7 cups (1.7 L) of water and boil until the potatoes are tender. Check them with a fork to make sure they are soft inside. When done, rinse the potatoes under cold water; the skins should peel off easily. Mash the potatoes until smooth, add the potato starch and stir to form a dough. If the dough feels too sticky to shape, add more potato starch.

To prepare the stuffing, heat the olive oil in a sauté pan over medium-high heat. Add the onion, stir and cook for 5 minutes. Add the mushrooms and cook for another 5 minutes. Finally, add the lentils, and salt and pepper to taste and cook for 2 minutes. Set aside to cool.

To form the cakes, take about 3 tablespoons (45 ml) of the dough in your hand and press it into your palm. Place a spoonful of stuffing over the dough, close it by folding it over and shape into a round disk. Heat a thin layer of coconut oil in a skillet over medium heat and cook the potato cakes on both sides until they develop a golden brown crust, about 4 minutes per side.

PER SERVING (3 SERVINGS): 744 Calories; 10 g Fat (11.5% calories from fat); 17 g Protein; 157 g Carbohydrate; 15 g Dietary Fiber; 0 mg Cholesterol; 48 mg Sodium

BLACK BEAN HUMMUS PANINI

I have a thing for grilled sandwiches, and with healthy, power-packed options like this one, I don't need to hold back. Hummus works very well when cooked in sandwiches, or even as a pizza topping in lieu of cheese. Aside from bringing in a protein component, hummus does a good job keeping the sandwich together and deepening the taste of eggplant and black beans. Use your favorite gluten-free, vegan bread for this recipe, or you can always go to the Quinoa Avocado Bread recipe (page 159).

Serves 1

4 thin eggplant slices

¼ cup (62 g) hummus

2 slices of your favorite gluten-free vegan bread

Salt

⅓ cup (57 g) cooked black beans

2 tbsp (7 g) sun-dried tomatoes

Vegan butter

Grill the eggplant slices in a pan or in a panini press until they are soft, about 5 minutes. Spread the hummus on one side of both slices of bread. Arrange the eggplant atop one layer of hummus and add a pinch of salt. Add the black beans and a little more salt over them. Add the sun-dried tomatoes. Top the sandwich with the second slice of bread and spread the vegan butter on the top of that slice. Grill the assembled sandwich in a panini press if you have one, or simply cook both sides of the sandwich in a pan while pressing, until the bread starts to brown and the ingredients are warm, about 4 minutes.

PER TOTAL RECIPE: 475 Calories; 9 g Fat (16.5% calories from fat); 24 g Protein; 78 g Carbohydrate; 16 g Dietary Fiber; 1 mg Cholesterol; 784 mg Sodium

BBQ JACKFRUIT WITH RED CABBAGE SLAW

Jackfruit, with its chewy, shredded, meaty texture and incredible flavor-absorbing properties makes for an enticing option for creative sandwiches. Here, it is combined with beans to introduce additional protein, flavored with BBQ sauce and spices and paired with a red cabbage slaw to freshen things up.

Serves 4

Rubbing Mixture

½ tsp chili powder

¼ tsp cayenne pepper

¼ tsp ground cumin

¼ tsp freshly ground black pepper

¼ tsp salt

1 tbsp (15 g) brown sugar

Jackfruit

1 (8-oz [225-g]) can jackfruit, drained and rinsed

2 tbsp (30 ml) olive oil

1 medium red onion, diced

2 cloves garlic, minced

½ cup (120 ml) vegan BBQ sauce

1 (15-oz [425-g]) can kidney beans, drained and rinsed

Red Cabbage Slaw

2 cups (680 g) thinly sliced red cabbage

1 tbsp (15 ml) freshly squeezed lemon or lime juice

1 tbsp (15 ml) olive oil

¼ tsp salt

¼ tsp granulated sugar

In a small bowl, combine all the rubbing mixture ingredients. Remove and discard the center core of the jackfruit, then rub the fruit with the rubbing mixture and set aside.

Heat the olive oil in a deep pot over medium-high heat. Add the onion and garlic and cook for 3 minutes. Add the jackfruit and cook, stirring, for another minute before adding the BBQ sauce. Lower the heat to medium-low, cover the pot and let simmer for 25 minutes. Finally, add the beans and cook for another 10 minutes.

To make the red cabbage slaw, in a bowl, combine all the slaw ingredients and massage with your fingers. The combination of the jackfruit and slaw makes for a great sandwich with a gluten-free, vegan bread or a wrap in a tortilla.

PER SERVING (4 SERVINGS): 308 Calories; 12 g Fat (33.4% calories from fat); 8 g Protein; 46 g Carbohydrate; 7 g Dietary Fiber; 0 mg Cholesterol; 860 mg Sodium

ARTICHOKE SALAD

Savory, sweet, spicy and tart, creamy, crunchy and chewy, all play together so deliciously in this salad. Not so much a salad in the green sense but it is a well-balanced, energizing meal. The serving suggestion is a sandwich and the recipe will make enough for a few of them. You will appreciate having this at the ready for a quick and filling meal option.

Serves 3

1 (15-oz [425-g]) can chickpeas, drained and rinsed

12 oz (340 g) marinated artichokes, drained

½ cup (115 g) vegan mayonnaise

1 tbsp (15 ml) cider vinegar

1 tsp (4 g) Dijon mustard

1 tbsp (9 g) capers

¼ tsp garlic powder

¼ tsp red pepper flakes

Salt and freshly ground black pepper

2 stalks celery, chopped

1 cup (20 g) arugula

¼ cup (35 g) pumpkin seeds

¼ cup (30 g) dried cranberries

2 tbsp (14 g) chopped roasted hazelnuts (optional)

Serving Suggestions

Gluten-free bread slices

Radish slices

Arugula

In a food processor, combine the chickpeas, artichokes, mayonnaise, vinegar, mustard, capers, garlic powder, red pepper flakes and salt and black pepper. Pulse a few times, transfer to a bowl and mix in the celery, arugula, pumpkin seeds, cranberries and hazelnuts. Serve in a sandwich along with radish slices and extra arugula.

PER SERVING (3 SERVINGS): 588 Calories; 37 g Fat (58.7% calories from fat); 11 g Protein; 47 g Carbohydrate; 14 g Dietary Fiber; 0 mg Cholesterol; 1061 mg Sodium

KALE, RED CABBAGE AND LENTIL SALAD

I love the combination of kale and red cabbage; they are so perfectly complementary. With a strong pairing like that to start with, not a whole lot more is needed to arrive at a great salad: pickles, parsley and a vegan mayo–based dressing to brighten it all up, plus green lentils to up the protein game. Nutritious, super simple and versatile.

Serves 2

Salad

1 cup (198 g) cooked green lentils

4 kale leaves, chopped

1 cup (80 g) shredded or chopped red cabbage

¼ cup (36 g) chopped cornichon pickles

¼ cup (15 g) chopped fresh parsley

Dressing

⅓ cup (75 g) vegan mayo

¼ tsp freshly ground black pepper

¼ tsp dried thyme

¼ tsp smoked paprika

¼ tsp garlic powder

⅛ tsp chili powder

1 ½ tsp (8 ml) balsamic or apple cider vinegar

In a large bowl, toss all the salad ingredients together. Mix the dressing ingredients together in a small bowl, add to the salad and toss again.

PER SERVING (3 SERVINGS): 384 Calories; 25 g Fat (61.6% calories from fat); 10 g Protein; 25 g Carbohydrate; 10 g Dietary Fiber; 0 mg Cholesterol; 360 mg Sodium

BLACK BEAN BURGERS

I love making my own wholesome, clean and nutritious veggie burger patties. This amazing patty is made from black beans, quinoa and pumpkin seeds, offering a load of protein and fiber along with a great form, taste and texture. You can keep the patties in the freezer, cooked or uncooked, for when that burger craving hits because it will hit when you taste this.

Serves 6

2 tbsp (30 ml) coconut oil (or any cooking oil), plus more to cook (optional)

¾ cup (120 g) finely diced onion (about ½ onion)

1 tbsp (7 g) ground cumin

1 ½ tsp (2 g) red pepper flakes

1 ½ tsp (4 g) smoked paprika

¾ cup (139 g) cooked quinoa

1 (15-oz [425-g]) can black beans, drained and rinsed

½ cup (70 g) roasted pumpkin seeds

1 tbsp (12 g) coconut sugar (or any sugar)

3 tbsp (45 ml) vegan BBQ sauce

Salt and freshly ground black pepper

½ cup (60 g) gluten-free vegan bread crumbs

Serving Suggestions

Gluten-free buns

Vegan mayo

Sliced Radishes

Pickled jalapeno

Arugula leaves

Avocado slices

Chopped red onion

Sprouts

Heat the oil in a skillet over medium heat, add the onion and cook for 2 minutes. Add the cumin, red pepper flakes and smoked paprika and cook for 5 minutes. Set aside to cool.

Once at room temperature, transfer to a food processor and add the rest of the ingredients. Pulse a few times to combine and break down the beans, but make sure not to process too much; leave some texture. Let the mixture chill in the fridge for about 20 minutes before shaping into patties.

Cook the patties in lightly oiled pan over medium heat until they develop a golden brown crust on both sides, about 5 minutes per side. Alternatively, bake for 25 minutes in an oven preheated to 350°F (175°C). Serve in a gluten-free bun with your favorite condiments. I used vegan mayo, radishes, pickled jalapeno, arugula leaves, avocado slices, red onion and sprouts.

PER SERVING (6 SERVINGS): 466 Calories; 9 g Fat (10.6% calories from fat); 20 g Protein; 79 g Carbohydrate; 13 g Dietary Fiber; 0 mg Cholesterol; 151 mg Sodium

QUINOA CREAM NOODLES

What if you could turn the protein powerhouse quinoa into a rich and creamy sauce that is perfect for noodles? Paired with broccoli, this dish is well balanced and energizing besides being incredibly tasty.

Serves 3

Quinoa Cream

1 ½ cups (278 g) cooked quinoa

1 cup (235 ml) almond milk

¼ cup (32 g) nutritional yeast

1 tsp (3 g) garlic powder

1 tsp (2 g) onion powder

1 tsp (4 g) Dijon mustard

1 tsp (2 g) dried oregano

1 tsp (1 g) dried thyme

Salt and freshly ground black pepper

Noodles

5 oz (142 g) uncooked gluten-free noodles

1 tbsp (15 ml) olive oil

3 cups (210 g) broccoli florets

Handful of arugula (optional)

In a high-speed blender, combine all the quinoa cream ingredients and blend until smooth, transfer to a container and set aside. Cook the noodles according to the package directions and set aside. Heat the olive oil in a large skillet and cook the broccoli florets for 3 minutes. Turn off the heat, add the noodles and stir. Serve with the quinoa cream and arugula.

PER SERVING (3 SERVINGS): 421 Calories; 11 g Fat (21.4% calories from fat); 18 g Protein; 71 g Carbohydrate; 10 g Dietary Fiber; 0 mg Cholesterol; 62 mg Sodium

BBQ BEAN LOAF

Rice and beans form the clean and complete protein basis of this well-seasoned, nourishing and satisfying loaf. The savory treat is complemented by a deliciously rich gravy sauce with its own kick of protein. This simple recipe this can easily be an entertaining favorite as well as provide a casual family meal.

Serves 3

Bean Loaf

2 tbsp (14 g) flaxseed meal

1 cup (128 g) cooked brown rice

1 (15-oz [425-g]) can kidney beans (or any other beans), drained and rinsed

4 green onions, chopped

½ cup (30 g) chopped fresh parsley

2 cloves garlic, minced

¼ cup (120 ml) vegan BBQ sauce

1 tbsp (7 g) ground cumin

1½ tsp (2 g) red pepper flakes

1½ tsp (4 g) smoked paprika

Salt and freshly ground black pepper

1 tbsp (15 ml) olive oil (or other cooking oil), plus more for pan

½ cup (60 g) gluten-free vegan bread crumbs

½ cup (55 g) chopped nuts (walnut, pecan, hazelnut)

Mushroom Gravy

¼ cup (60 ml) coconut oil or olive oil

½ cup (80 g) finely chopped onion

2 cloves garlic, minced

3 cups (210 g) finely chopped mushrooms

Salt and freshly ground black pepper

½ cup (63 g) garbanzo bean flour

2 cups (455 ml) vegetable stock

1 bay leaf

1 tsp (1 g) dried thyme

Preheat the oven to 400°F (200°C). In a small bowl, combine the flaxseed meal with ⅓ cup (80 ml) of water, mix well and let sit for 5 minutes. In a food processor, combine all the remaining bean loaf ingredients, except the nuts, and pulse a few times to mix, but leave some texture. Add the nuts and stir. Lightly oil a baking pan (I used a 5 x 7-inch [12.5 x 18-cm] pan), transfer the loaf mixture to the pan and bake for 25 minutes.

While it is baking, prepare the mushroom gravy by heating the oil in a large skillet over medium-high heat. Add the onion, garlic, mushrooms and salt and pepper to taste and cook, stirring, for 8 to 10 minutes. Sprinkle in the garbanzo bean flour while stirring and add the vegetable stock, bay leaf and thyme. Cook until the sauce thickens. Slice and serve the bean loaf hot, topped with the mushroom gravy.

PER SERVING (3 SERVINGS): 1217 Calories; 44 g Fat (31.6% calories from fat); 55 g Protein; 160 g Carbohydrate; 47 g Dietary Fiber; 2 mg Cholesterol; 1436 mg Sodium

OVEN-ROASTED SUMMER VEGGIES

Summer immediately reminds me of tomatoes, peppers and eggplants. Each is absolutely delicious by itself but when they are combined, things become Mediterranean really fast. I also incorporated kidney beans into this oven roast for added texture and protein. This one is an easy dish to make and it can be enjoyed hot or cold. I usually make enough of it to last for a few days and I use it stand alone, over rice, on toasts, in sandwiches, etc. . . . Definitely very versatile, colorful, nutritious and yummy.

Serves 3

1 red bell pepper, chopped

2 medium tomatoes, wedge sliced

½ large or 1 small eggplant, chopped

1 large or 2 small zucchinis, chopped

2 shallots, chopped

1 cup (60 g) cooked kidney beans (or use from can)

2 stalks green garlic, roughly chopped

Salt, ground black pepper and rosemary, to taste

2 tbsp (30 ml) olive oil

Serving Suggestions
Fresh arugula

Hummus

Hemp seeds

Preheat the oven to 400°F (200°C). Place all the veggies, the kidney beans and green garlic in an oven pan (I used a 10-inch [25.4-cm] cast-iron pan). Add the salt, black pepper and the rosemary. Pour the olive oil over the veggies and mix. Cook in the oven for 40 minutes, stirring 2 times in between. I served the vegetables over a bed of fresh arugula, topped with hummus and sprinkled with hemp seeds.

PER SERVING (3 SERVINGS): 413 Calories; 14 g Fat (28.4% calories from fat); 17 g Protein; 61 g Carbohydrate; 18 g Dietary Fiber; 0 mg Cholesterol; 33 mg Sodium

ZUCCHINI NOODLES WITH GARLIC AVOCADO SAUCE

Zucchini noodles, affectionately called "zoodles," are a healthy and fiber-rich alternative to pasta. The garlic avocado sauce with hemp seeds introduces the healthy fats and protein to balance out and deliciously flavor this green goodness.

Serves 3

3 to 4 medium zucchini

1 tbsp (15 ml) olive oil

1 (15-oz [425-g]) can white beans, drained and rinsed

Avocado Sauce

1 ripe avocado, pitted and peeled

1 tbsp (15 ml) olive oil

½ cup (30 g) chopped fresh parsley or ½ cup (40 g) basil

Juice of ½ lemon or lime

1 to 2 cloves garlic, minced

Salt and freshly ground black pepper

Serving Suggestions

Purple carrot slices

Fresh thyme

Hemp seeds

Cut off and discard the zucchini ends. Use a spiralizer or peeler to make zucchini noodles. Heat the olive oil in a skillet over high heat, add the zucchini and beans and cook, stirring, for 1 minute. In a food processor, combine all the avocado sauce ingredients and pulse a few times to get to the texture you like. Mix together the sauce, zucchini and beans and serve.

PER SERVING (3 SERVINGS): 388 Calories; 20 g Fat (43.9% calories from fat); 14 g Protein; 43 g Carbohydrate; 11 g Dietary Fiber; 0 mg Cholesterol; 25 mg Sodium

WHITE BEAN GRATIN

A easy cashew-based béchamel works wonders, turning a load of vegetables and beans into a hearty, fulfilling, protein- and fiber-rich meal. This was an instant family favorite.

Serves 4

2 tbsp (30 ml) olive oil or coconut oil

1 medium onion, chopped

2 cloves garlic, minced

1 jalapeño pepper, seeded and chopped

2 stalks celery, sliced

1 carrot, chopped

3 medium potatoes, chopped

2 tbsp (32 g) tomato paste

1 bay leaf

Salt and freshly ground black pepper

1 (15-oz [425-g]) can white beans, drained and rinsed

Béchamel Sauce

⅓ cup (47 g) raw cashews (preferably soaked in water for 4 hours or overnight)

½ cup (120 ml) plant-based milk

¼ cup (32 g) nutritional yeast

1 tsp (3 g) garlic powder

1 tsp (1 g) dried thyme

Serving Suggestions

½ cup (30 g) chopped fresh parsley

Cooked white rice

Preheat the oven to 350°F (175°C). Heat the coconut oil in a large cast-iron skillet or Dutch oven over medium heat, add the onion and cook for 5 minutes. Add the garlic, jalapeño, celery, carrot and potatoes and cook for 2 more minutes. Add the tomato paste along with 1 cup (235 ml) of water, the bay leaf and salt and pepper to taste and cook for 15 minutes. Add the white beans and cook, stirring, for another 15 minutes. In a high-speed blender, combine all the béchamel sauce ingredients and blend until smooth. Pour the sauce over the bean mixture and place in the oven. Bake for 15 minutes. Top with chopped parsley and optionally serve alongside white rice.

PER SERVING (4 SERVINGS): 657 Calories; 15 g Fat (19.9% calories from fat); 36 g Protein; 101 g Carbohydrate; 24 g Dietary Fiber; 0 mg Cholesterol; 137 mg Sodium

RED BELL PEPPER CHICKPEA PASTA

The combination of mildly sweet red bell peppers, tomatoes and chickpeas is a winner in all the fronts of taste, texture and nutrition. When in a time crunch, whip up this quick recipe and enjoy that happy tummy feeling.

Serves 3

8 oz (227 g) gluten-free pasta

2 tbsp (30 ml) olive oil

2 red bell peppers, diced

3 cloves garlic, minced

1 cup (180 g) diced tomato

2 tbsp (32 g) tomato paste

¼ tsp red pepper flakes

¼ tsp dried thyme

Salt and freshly ground black pepper

1 (15-oz [425-g]) can chickpeas, drained and rinsed

Optional Toppings

Basil leaves

Hemp seeds

Cook the pasta according to the package directions, drain and set aside. Heat the olive oil in a skillet over medium-low heat, add the bell peppers and cook for 15 minutes, or until the peppers caramelize. Add the garlic, tomato, tomato paste, red pepper flakes, thyme and salt and black pepper to taste and cook for 5 minutes. Finally, add the chickpeas and cook for another 5 minutes. Transfer to a food processor and pulse a few times to coarsely break down the mixture. Serve over the pasta, topped (if using) with basil leaves and hemp seeds.

PER SERVING (3 SERVINGS): 554 Calories; 14 g Fat (21.1% calories from fat); 15 g Protein; 100 g Carbohydrate; 10 g Dietary Fiber; 0 mg Cholesterol; 524 mg Sodium

POLENTA PIZZA

Polenta has a deep capacity to soak up flavors and bring them out in a whole new way. That's why it makes a lot of sense to use it as an easy pizza crust, topped with fragrant basil and sweet peas with the added texture and earthy flavor of nuts. Every layer of this pizza introduces a different, healthy source of protein, through the polenta itself, hazelnuts, peas and hemp seeds.

Serves 4

Crust

18 oz (510 g) precooked polenta

1 tbsp (15 ml) olive oil, plus more for pan

½ tsp dried thyme

½ tsp freshly ground black pepper

½ tsp hot sauce

½ tsp salt

Sauce

1 avocado, pitted and peeled

1 cup (40 g) packed basil leaves

2 cloves garlic

¼ cup (60 ml) olive oil

⅓ cup (38 g) roasted hazelnuts (or any nut)

Juice of ½ lime

Toppings

½ cup (75 g) peas, cooked

3 small sweet peppers, sliced

A few grape tomatoes

Handful of arugula

2 tbsp (22 g) hemp seeds

Preheat the oven to 350°F (175°C). Crumble the polenta into a medium bowl, add the rest of the crust ingredients and mix well. Evenly spread the polenta crust in the bottom of cast-iron pan (or baking dish) lightly coated with oil. Bake for 20 minutes. In the meantime, in a food processor, combine all the sauce ingredients and pulse a few times, leaving a somewhat coarse texture. Remove the baked polenta crust from the oven and let cool. Spread the sauce over the crust, add the toppings and serve.

PER SERVING (4 SERVINGS): 447 Calories; 33 g Fat (64.2% calories from fat); 10 g Protein; 32 g Carbohydrate; 5 g Dietary Fiber; 0 mg Cholesterol; 687 mg Sodium

BROCCOLI QUINOA WRAP WITH AVOCADO PESTO

Get your greens, grains and healthy fats in a wrap with this incredibly delicious combination of several superfoods. The zesty pesto is made smooth and creamy by using avocado and complements the filling perfectly. I can't have enough of this.

Serves 2

Filling

½ cup (87 g) uncooked quinoa, rinsed

½ cup (98 g) uncooked rice

2 tbsp (30 ml) olive oil

4 cups (284 g) broccoli florets

1 tsp (2 g) Italian seasoning

½ tsp garlic powder

Salt and freshly ground black pepper

Avocado Pesto

1 ripe avocado, pitted and peeled

1 cup (40 g) packed fresh basil leaves

½ cup (90 g) hemp seeds

3 cloves garlic, minced

Juice of ½ lemon

Salt and freshly ground black pepper

¼ cup (60 ml) olive oil

Serving

2 gluten-free tortillas

In a medium pot, combine the quinoa and rice with 3 cups (710 ml) of water, bring to a boil and let simmer for 20 minutes. Meanwhile, heat the olive oil in a sauté pan over medium-high heat. Add the broccoli florets, Italian seasoning, garlic powder and salt and pepper to taste and cook for 5 minutes.

To make the avocado pesto, in a food processor, combine all the pesto ingredients, except the olive oil. Pulse a few times to mix and break down, leaving a coarse texture. Add the olive oil and pulse one more time to incorporate. Drain the quinoa mixture and combine with the avocado pesto. Wrap it all together with the cooked broccoli in gluten-free tortillas.

PER SERVING (2 SERVINGS): 1320 Calories; 83 g Fat (55.5% calories from fat); 36 g Protein; 114 g Carbohydrate; 17 g Dietary Fiber; 0 mg Cholesterol; 404 mg Sodium

TOASTED CHICKPEA TACOS WITH MANGO RELISH

Sweet and zesty, and smooth and spicy, these are incredibly flavorful and playful, just like how proper tacos should be.

Serves 3

Toasted Chickpeas

1 tbsp (15 ml) olive oil

1 (15-oz [425-g]) can chickpeas, drained and rinsed

1 tsp (3 g) ground cumin

1 tsp (2 g) garam masala

¼ tsp red pepper flakes

Salt

Tahini Sauce

⅓ cup (80 g) tahini

2 tbsp (8 g) finely chopped fresh dill

2 tbsp (30 ml) apple cider vinegar

½ tsp red pepper flakes

¼ tsp freshly ground black pepper

2 cloves garlic, minced

½ tsp salt

Mango Relish

½ mango, peeled, pitted and cubed

2 tsp (10 ml) cider vinegar

2 tsp (1 g) finely chopped fresh cilantro

¼ tsp red pepper flakes

Pinch of salt

Taco

Soft gluten-free corn tortillas

Handful of arugula

½ red onion, sliced

1 avocado, pitted, peeled and sliced

Red pepper flakes

Heat the olive oil in a large sauté pan over medium-high heat, add the chickpeas and spices and cook, stirring, for 5 minutes; set aside. In a small bowl, stir together all the tahini sauce ingredients along with ¼ cup (60 ml) of water and set aside. In a separate bowl, mix together all the mango relish ingredients. Warm the tortillas in a dry skillet or directly over your stovetop burner. Top the tortillas with arugula leaves, toasted chickpeas, mango relish, red onion and avocado slices. Drizzle with tahini sauce, sprinkle with red pepper flakes and serve.

PER SERVING (3 SERVINGS): 1180 Calories; 45 g Fat (33.9% calories from fat); 32 g Protein; 167 g Carbohydrate; 19 g Dietary Fiber; 0 mg Cholesterol; 1793 mg Sodium

QUINOA CHILI

Chili is a trusty way of getting a load of plant proteins and fiber. This quick chili recipe not only improves the practicality, but also ups the nutrition game with quinoa. Enjoy the warmth of this robust, spicy, comforting dish anytime on a whim.

Serves 4

⅔ cup (116 g) uncooked quinoa, rinsed

1 tbsp (15 ml) olive or coconut oil

1 medium red onion, diced

2 cloves garlic, minced

2 tsp (5 g) ground cumin

1 tsp (3 g) smoked paprika

1 tsp (1 g) red pepper flakes

1 jalapeño pepper, seeded and diced

1 red bell pepper

1 cup (180 g) diced tomato
(2 medium tomatoes)

1 tbsp (16 g) tomato paste

½ cup (120 ml) vegan vegetable stock

½ tsp coconut sugar or any sugar

2 tsp (5 g) unsweetened cocoa powder

1 (15-oz [425-g]) can kidney beans, drained and rinsed

1 (15-oz [425-g]) can black beans, drained and rinsed

Salt and freshly ground black pepper

Cook the quinoa according to the package directions and set aside. Heat the olive oil in a large skillet, preferably cast iron, over medium heat. Add the onion, garlic and spices and sauté for 5 minutes. Add the jalapeño and bell peppers, tomato, tomato paste, vegetable stock, sugar and cocoa powder. Mix well and cook for 5 minutes. Add the quinoa and beans and season with salt and black pepper to taste. Cook for 5 more minutes and serve warm.

PER SERVING (4 SERVINGS): 386 Calories; 7 g Fat (17% calories from fat); 18 g Protein; 64 g Carbohydrate; 17 g Dietary Fiber; trace Cholesterol; 939 mg Sodium

PESTO PIZZA WITH A RICE AND GREEN LENTIL CRUST

I am quite fond of this recipe, featuring a zesty pesto spread over a brown rice and green lentil crust. It is absolutely delicious, protein- and fiber-rich, and so ridiculously simple. I loved, loved the texture and taste of this one. It holds together beautifully and is just a joy to devour.

Serves 4

Crust

1 cup (200 g) dried green lentils

1 cup (190 g) uncooked brown rice, sprouted (soak the raw rice in water for 1 day)

¼ cup (60 ml) olive oil

2 tbsp (32 g) tomato paste

1 tsp (3 g) garlic powder

1 tsp (1 g) dried thyme

¾ tsp salt

Pesto

3 cups (120 g) fresh basil leaves

⅓ cup (48 g) almonds (or another nut of your choice)

3 large cloves garlic

¼ cup (32 g) nutritional yeast (optional)

¼ tsp salt, or to taste

¼ tsp freshly ground black pepper

⅓ cup (80 ml) olive oil

Suggested Toppings

Red bell pepper

Pickled jalapeño peppers

Sliced cherry tomatoes

Capers

Fresh basil leaves

To make the crust, in a large pot, combine the lentils and rice along with enough water to cover. Bring to a boil and let cook for 10 minutes. The mixture should be cooked through but still firm. Drain the water, transfer the mixture to a food processor and add the rest of the crust ingredients (depending on the size of your food processor, you may need to do this step in two batches). Process until the mixture reaches a firm, doughlike consistency. It won't turn completely smooth; there will still be some texture due to the rice and the lentils, but it shouldn't be too coarse.

Preheat the oven to 350°F (175°C). On a large piece of parchment paper, spread out the dough into an approximately 10-inch (25.5 cm)-diameter pie with a raised rim. Transfer the crust to the oven together with the parchment paper (I cooked mine over a pizza stone, but if you don't have that, you can use a baking sheet beneath the paper) and bake for 15 minutes. Remove from the oven and let the crust cool while you work on the pesto topping.

In a food processor, combine all the pesto ingredients, except the olive oil, and process until you are happy with the texture. Transfer to a bowl and mix in the olive oil.

Spread the pesto uniformly over the baked crust and add the suggested toppings or your favorite toppings.

PER SERVING (4 SERVINGS): 634 Calories; 40 g Fat (55.2% calories from fat); 16 g Protein; 57 g Carbohydrate; 10 g Dietary Fiber; 0 mg Cholesterol; 609 mg Sodium

AVOCADO PESTO SPAGHETTI

Whenever I am in doubt about what to eat, I go to avocado pesto because it is beautiful and fragrant and delicious and nutritious, but also because I almost always have these simple ingredients on hand. Besides the use as a spaghetti sauce, this pesto works great as a dip or over toast.

Serves 2

8 oz (226 g) gluten-free pasta

Pesto

1 ripe avocado, pitted and peeled

1 cup (40 g) packed fresh basil leaves

2 to 3 cloves garlic, minced

⅓ cup (60 g) hemp seeds

Juice of ½ lime

Salt and freshly ground black pepper

2 tbsp (30 ml) olive oil

Toppings

Hemp seeds

Roasted hazelnuts, crushed

Roasted red and yellow bell peppers (optional)

Cook the spaghetti according to the package directions, drain and set aside. In a food processor, combine all the pesto ingredients, except the olive oil, and pulse a few times to mix and break down. Adjust the texture to your liking, but do not overprocess. Add the olive oil and pulse a few more times to incorporate. Serve with the cooked spaghetti and garnish with the toppings.

PER SERVING (2 SERVINGS): 790 Calories; 40 g Fat (43.5% calories from fat); 22 g Protein; 96 g Carbohydrate; 8 g Dietary Fiber; 0 mg Cholesterol; 16 mg Sodium

BUCKWHEAT NOODLES WITH SAUTÉED VEGETABLES

Buckwheat noodles (a.k.a. soba noodles) have a lot going for them. They are very flavorful and firm. They are not very starchy, so they are just as good cold as when they are hot. I love the magical flavor combination of these noodles with portobello mushrooms and soy sauce. The peas bring in some sweetness to balance things out and the carrots bring in a nice texture. My version has a few Mediterranean elements as well.

Serves 2

1 (8.8-oz [249-g]) package gluten-free soba noodles

1 tbsp (15 ml) olive oil

1 shallot, chopped, or ¼ cup (40 g) chopped onion

1 carrot, diced

1 cup (150 g) peas

6 medium portobello mushrooms, sliced

3 kale leaves, stemmed and chopped

2 cloves garlic, minced

1 tsp (3 g) grated fresh ginger

3 tbsp (45 ml) coconut aminos

2 tbsp (30 ml) rice vinegar

Optional Garnishes

Sesame seeds

Chopped fresh parsley

Shredded red cabbage

Cook the soba noodles according to the package directions. Heat the olive oil in a skillet over medium heat, add the shallot and cook for 2 minutes. Add the carrot and peas and cook for 3 more minutes. Add the mushrooms, kale, garlic, ginger, coconut aminos and vinegar and cook for 4 minutes. Finally, add the noodles and cook for another minute. Serve (if using) with sesame seeds, chopped parsley and shredded red cabbage.

PER SERVING (2 SERVINGS): 659 Calories; 10 g Fat (13.7% calories from fat); 39 g Protein; 106 g Carbohydrate; 16 g Dietary Fiber; 0 mg Cholesterol; 2583 mg Sodium

VEGGIE CAKES WITH GARBANZO BEAN FLOUR

These savory cakes feature a hefty portion of vegetables together with the protein-packed garbanzo bean flour and make for a great on-the-go snack or side.

Serves 4

Batter

1½ cups (188 g) garbanzo bean flour

¼ cup (32 g) nutritional yeast

½ tsp baking soda

¼ tsp sea salt

¼ tsp freshly ground black pepper

Veggie Mixture

1 tbsp (15 ml) coconut or olive oil, plus more for muffin cups

½ red onion, chopped

1 clove garlic, minced

1 tsp (2.5 g) ground cumin

1 tsp (2 g) dried oregano

½ tsp red pepper flakes

3 cups (about 370 g) fresh or frozen mixed vegetables (I used broccoli, cauliflower, carrots, green beans)

Salt and freshly ground black pepper

Preheat the oven to 400°F (200°C). In a bowl, mix the batter ingredients with 2 cups (475 ml) of water and set aside. To make the veggie mixture, heat the coconut oil in a sauté pan over medium-high heat. Add the onion, garlic, cumin, oregano and red pepper flakes and cook for 3 minutes. Add the mixed vegetables and salt and black pepper to taste and cook for another 3 minutes. Brush 8 muffin cups with oil, fill halfway with the veggie mixture and top evenly with the batter. Bake for 30 to 35 minutes, or until a toothpick poked in the center of the cakes comes out clean. Remove from the oven and allow to cool for 10 minutes before transferring to a wire rack. Serve warm or cold.

PER SERVING (3 SERVINGS): 277 Calories; 5 g Fat (16.0% calories from fat); 20 g Protein; 42 g Carbohydrate; 13 g Dietary Fiber; 0 mg Cholesterol; 441 mg Sodium

BEAN AND CAULIFLOWER RICE TACOS

A fresh and wholesome take on tacos with baked spicy cauliflower rice and beans, along with other beautiful and delicious toppings. Tacos are always a great option for a quickly put together, fun and filling meal. It's a win-win situation when a festive comfort food is also nutritionally balanced and powerful.

Serves 4

1 medium cauliflower, separated into florets, or 3 cups (300 g) cauliflower rice

Bean Mixture

1 (15-oz [425-g]) can kidney beans, drained and rinsed

2 tbsp (32 g) tomato paste

2 tbsp (16 g) nutritional yeast

1 tsp (2 g) onion powder

½ tsp garlic powder

½ tsp dried oregano

¼ tsp cayenne pepper

Salt and freshly ground black pepper

Tacos

4 or more gluten-free tortillas (depending on how large they are)

1 avocado, peeled, pitted and mashed

1 cup (70 g) thinly sliced red cabbage

2 small radishes, sliced

Handful of arugula

Preheat the oven to 425°F (220°C). Line a baking sheet with parchment paper and set aside. If using cauliflower florets, place them in a food processor and pulse until you get a rice-like texture. Transfer the cauliflower rice to a large bowl. In the food processor, combine all the bean mixture ingredients and pulse a few times to break down and combine, leaving some texture. Combine the bean mixture with the cauliflower rice. Spread the mixture on the parchment paper and bake for 8 minutes. Serve in taco shells or tortillas along with avocado, red cabbage, radish and arugula.

PER SERVING (4 SERVINGS): 714 Calories; 13 g Fat (12.4% calories from fat); 40 g Protein; 115 g Carbohydrate; 43 g Dietary Fiber; 0 mg Cholesterol; 520 mg Sodium

CURRIED RED LENTILS

I love spicy food and that very much reflects in my cooking. I just think spices hold almost magical powers to absolutely transform recipes, develop deeper lingering tastes and open up entirely new possibilities. This nourishing red lentil curry is a protein and fiber powerhouse, besides being a perfect, warming comfort food. In combination, the red lentils and the coconut cream absorb and bring out a wonderfully deep and satisfying curry flavor.

Serves 4

2 tbsp (30 ml) coconut oil or olive oil

1 medium onion, chopped

2 cloves garlic, minced

1 tbsp (8 g) grated fresh ginger

1 tbsp (7 g) curry powder

2 tbsp (32 g) tomato paste

½ tsp red pepper flakes

¾ cup (121 g) chopped tomato

4 cups (946 ml) vegetable stock or water

1½ cups (300 g) dried red lentils, rinsed

1 bay leaf (optional)

Salt and freshly ground black pepper

1 (14-oz [414-ml]) can coconut cream or coconut milk

Serving Suggestions

Mixed greens

Micro greens

Gluten-free flatbread (page 160)

Heat the coconut oil in a pot over medium heat. Add the onion and cook for about 3 minutes. Add the garlic and ginger and cook for 2 more minutes. Add the curry powder, tomato paste, red pepper flakes and tomato and cook, stirring, for 3 minutes. Add the vegetable stock, red lentils, bay leaf (if using), and salt and black pepper to taste, and cook for about 20 minutes. Finally, add the coconut cream and cook, stirring, for another 2 minutes, until the cream melts and is incorporated. Serve it topped with micro greens, alongside mixed greens and gluten-free flatbread.

PER SERVING (4 SERVINGS): 686 Calories; 48 g Fat (59.5% calories from fat); 18 g Protein; 55 g Carbohydrate; 13 g Dietary Fiber; 2 mg Cholesterol; 1703 mg Sodium

GENERAL TSO'S CHICKPEAS

With the addition of a sweet and tangy flavor you came to love in the Asian cuisine, chickpeas are transformed into a comfort food that is loaded with protein and fiber. The best part is, it is surprisingly fast and easy.

Serves 3

1 (15-oz [425-g]) can chickpeas, drained and rinsed

¼ cup (32 g) arrowroot starch or cornstarch

3 tbsp (45 ml) coconut oil or sesame oil

2 cloves garlic, minced

1½ tsp (4 g) grated fresh ginger

2 tbsp (30 ml) pure maple syrup

2 tbsp (30 ml) coconut aminos

2 tbsp (30 ml) ketchup

1 tsp (5 ml) hot sauce

3 green onions, sliced

¾ cup (175 ml) vegetable stock

Serving Suggestions

Gluten-free noodles or rice

Chopped parsley

Coat the chickpeas with the starch by tossing in a bowl. Heat the coconut oil in a skillet over medium-high heat, add the coated chickpeas and cook, stirring, for 3 minutes. Add the remaining ingredients in order while stirring and cook for 5 more minutes, or until the sauce thickens. Serve hot, along with gluten-free noodles or rice, topped with chopped parsley.

PER SERVING (3 SERVINGS): 797 Calories; 24 g Fat (25.9% calories from fat); 30 g Protein; 121 g Carbohydrate; 27 g Dietary Fiber; 1 mg Cholesterol; 784 mg Sodium

MUNG BEAN PANCAKES

Mung beans are an excellent source of protein, and are cherished in the Indian and Asian cuisines despite being relatively obscure in Western cuisines. These tasty little green ones have quite the playful texture, leading to these amazing savory pancakes.

Serves 3

½ cup (100 g) dried green mung beans

¼ cup (49 g) uncooked white rice

2 green onions, finely sliced

½ cup (30 g) chopped fresh parsley

½ cup (32 g) chopped fresh dill

¼ cup (32 g) nutritional yeast

Salt and freshly ground black pepper

1 tbsp (15 ml) olive oil

Soak the mung beans and rice together in water overnight. Drain and rinse. In a high-speed blender, combine the mung bean mixture with ¼ cup (60 ml) of water and blend to the consistency of regular pancake batter; add more water if it remains too thick. Transfer to a bowl and stir in the rest of the ingredients, except the olive oil. Heat the olive oil in a skillet over medium-high heat and pour in a few spoonfuls of the batter, depending on how large you prefer the pancakes. Cook on both sides until you get a golden brown crust, then repeat with the rest of the batter.

PER SERVING (3 SERVINGS): 191 Calories; 6 g Fat (26.7% calories from fat); 11 g Protein; 27 g Carbohydrate; 8 g Dietary Fiber; 0 mg Cholesterol; 18 mg Sodium

QUINOA FALAFEL

A combination of Mediterranean and Mexican cuisines, this recipe combines the best of both worlds with nutritious, protein-packed quinoa-chickpea falafel served in tacos along with a cilantro tahini sauce. This is just a blast, either for entertaining or keeping it all to yourself. You know you want to try it.

Serves 4

Falafel

4 green onions, chopped

2 cloves garlic, minced

1 cup (60 g) chopped fresh parsley

1 cup (185 g) cooked quinoa

½ cup (60 g) gluten-free vegan bread crumbs

1 (15-oz [425-g]) can chickpeas, drained and rinsed

2 tbsp (32 g) tomato paste

2 tbsp (30 ml) olive oil

1 tbsp (15 ml) cider vinegar

1 tsp (1 g) red pepper flakes

1½ tsp (4 g) ground cumin

½ tsp dried thyme

¼ tsp freshly ground black pepper

2 tbsp (16 g) sesame seeds (optional, for coating)

Grapeseed oil for frying

Cilantro Tahini Sauce

¼ cup (60 g) tahini

Juice of ½ lime

2 cloves garlic, crushed

2 tsp (10 ml) cider vinegar

½ tsp grated fresh ginger

¼ tsp salt

2 tsp (1 g) finely chopped fresh cilantro

Serving Suggestions

Soft corn taco shells

Arugula leaves

Roasted red bell peppers

Sliced red onion

Sliced radishes

In a food processor, combine all the falafel ingredients, except the sesame seeds and grapeseed oil, and process until it turns into a sticky mixture with a moderately coarse texture. Shape into 1.5-inch (4-cm)-diameter balls and let chill in the fridge for about 20 minutes. As an optional step, sprinkle the balls with the sesame seeds. In a medium saucepan or preferably a cast-iron skillet, heat about a 2-inch (5-cm) depth of grapeseed oil over medium-high heat. Make sure the falafel balls are sizzling when dipped in the oil. Fry the falafel in batches, without overcrowding and cooling down the oil, until they develop a golden brown crust.

To make the sauce, in a small bowl simply mix all the sauce ingredients with ⅓ cup (80 ml) of water and serve with the falafel. I serve the falafels in soft corn taco shells, with arugula, roasted red peppers, red onion slices and radishes.

PER SERVING (4 SERVINGS): 712 Calories; 25 g Fat (30.6% calories from fat); 27 g Protein; 100 g Carbohydrate; 23 g Dietary Fiber; 0 mg Cholesterol; 392 mg Sodium

BIRYANI

A classic from Indian cuisine, this fragrant rice dish is a huge favorite among many. The recipe is simplified from the traditional version, but no sacrifices were made in deliciousness. It's spicy without being overwhelming, and has a hefty portion of vegetables. Together with the protein-packed goodness of the rice and peas combination, it makes for a great option as a bring-along workday lunch as well as a comforting family dinner.

Serves 3

1 cup (190 g) uncooked basmati rice, rinsed

1 bay leaf

Salt and freshly ground black pepper

Pinch of saffron (optional)

2 tbsp (30 ml) coconut oil

1 medium yellow onion, diced finely

2 cloves garlic, minced

1 tsp (2.7 g) grated fresh ginger

2 tsp (4 g) garam masala

½ tsp ground cumin

½ tsp ground coriander

¼ tsp red pepper flakes

⅛ tsp ground turmeric

2 tbsp (32 g) tomato paste

2 medium tomatoes, diced

1 red bell pepper, chopped

½ medium cauliflower, cut into florets

1 cup (150 g) peas

Salt and black pepper

¼ cup (35 g) roasted cashews

¼ cup (35 g) dried wild blueberries or raisins

¼ cup (35 g) roasted pumpkin seeds (optional)

Optional Garnishes
Chopped fresh cilantro, for serving

Lime slices, for serving

Cook the rice according to the package directions, adding the bay leaf, salt and pepper while it is cooking. In the meantime, in a small bowl, mix the saffron (if using) with 2 tablespoons (30 ml) of hot water and set aside.

Heat the coconut oil in a large skillet over medium heat. Add the onion and cook for 5 minutes. Add the garlic, ginger and all the spices and cook, stirring, for 1 more minute before adding the tomato paste and the vegetables along with ½ cup (120 ml) of water. Add salt and black pepper to taste and cook for 5 minutes. Turn off the heat and mix in the cooked rice–saffron mixture (if using), cashews, wild blueberries and pumpkin seeds (if using). Serve hot, topped with chopped cilantro and lime slices (if using).

PER SERVING (3 SERVINGS): 523 Calories; 18 g Fat (29.2% calories from fat); 15 g Protein; 81 g Carbohydrate; 10 g Dietary Fiber; 0 mg Cholesterol; 177 mg Sodium

COCONUT CASHEW KORMA

Another Indian favorite, this korma derives its luxurious creaminess from the combination of cashews and coconut cream. It is mildly sweet and properly spiced up for a warming depth. Pair with brown rice to complement both the taste and the protein profile.

Serves 3

¾ cup (105 g) raw cashews (preferably soaked in water for at least 4 hours)

1 (14-oz [397-g]) can coconut cream or coconut milk

2 tbsp (30 ml) coconut oil

1 onion, diced

2 cloves garlic, minced

2 tsp (5 g) ground cumin

2 tsp (4 g) ground coriander

2 tsp (4 g) garam masala

2 tsp (4 g) curry powder

1½ tbsp (12 g) grated fresh ginger

½ tsp red pepper flakes

¼ tsp freshly ground black pepper

½ tsp ground turmeric

1 cup (180 g) diced tomato

2 cups (142 g) broccoli florets

1 cup (150 g) peas

1 bay leaf

Serving Suggestions

Cooked brown rice

Fresh cilantro leaves

Red pepper flakes

In a high-speed blender, combine the cashews, coconut cream and ½ cup (120 ml) of water and blend until smooth. Set aside. Heat the coconut oil in a large skillet over medium-high heat, add the onion, garlic and all the spices (but not the bay leaf yet) and cook, stirring, for 5 minutes. Add the tomato, broccoli and the peas and cook for another 5 minutes. Finally, add the cashew mixture along with the bay leaf and cook for 2 more minutes. Optionally serve over brown rice, topped with a few fresh cilantro leaves and red pepper flakes.

PER SERVING (3 SERVINGS): 838 Calories; 74 g Fat (74.4% calories from fat); 18 g Protein; 39 g Carbohydrate; 9 g Dietary Fiber; 0 mg Cholesterol; 41 mg Sodium

QUINOA TABBOULEH

Tabbouleh is one of my go-to meals. I love the goodness, the spiciness, the ease and the fact that it is enjoyable both hot and cold. It is essentially a superpowered salad and an excellent way to load up on beneficial grains. Traditionally made with fine bulgur, this gluten-free version swaps in quinoa, only to make things so much better.

Serves 4

3 kale leaves, stemmed and chopped

1 tsp (6 g) salt

1 cup (60 g) chopped fresh parsley

2 green onions, finely chopped

2 tbsp (30 ml) olive oil

3 tbsp (48 g) tomato paste

1 tbsp (15 ml) hot sauce

1 tsp (1 g) dried thyme

½ tsp freshly ground black pepper

2 cups (370 g) cooked quinoa

Juice of ½ lime

Serving Suggestions

4 gluten-free tortillas

½ cup (35 g) thinly sliced red cabbage

Handful of arugula

In a large bowl, combine the kale with the salt and massage with your fingers to soften the leaves. Add the parsley and green onions and set aside. Heat the olive oil in a large sauté pan over medium-high heat, add the tomato paste, hot sauce, thyme and pepper, and cook, stirring, for 2 minutes. Add the quinoa, stir and cook for 2 more minutes. Transfer to a bowl and let cool. When the quinoa mixture is at room temperature, add the kale mixture and the lime juice and combine. Serve as a salad, or as a salad wrap in tortillas with red cabbage and arugula. It will keep in the fridge for up to 3 days.

PER SERVING (4 SERVINGS): 193 Calories; 9 g Fat (40.7% calories from fat); 5 g Protein; 24 g Carbohydrate; 4 g Dietary Fiber; 0 mg Cholesterol; 743 mg Sodium

OLIVER SALAD

This is not really an ordinary potato salad in that it is meant to be enjoyed as an *amuse-bouche* component, a side dish, an appetizer or as a garnish to sandwiches. It just works so well for adding a rich taste and presence. My favorite way is to stuff baked potatoes with this, alongside some good old ketchup and other garnishes. The plant-based version, of course, removes the worry about cholesterol, letting you enjoy the benefits of the pea-potato protein duo.

Serves 4

4 medium potatoes

1 medium carrot, peeled

1 cup (130 g) frozen peas

½ cup (72 g) chopped cornichon pickles

1 cup (225 g) vegan mayo

1 tsp (4 g) Dijon mustard

Salt and freshly ground black pepper

Serving Suggestion

Baked sweet potato slices

In a saucepan, combine the potatoes, carrot and 6 cups (1.4 L) of water and boil until the potatoes are soft, 20 to 25 minutes. Add the peas and cook for a few more minutes, but take care not to overcook and turn them mushy. Drain the water and rinse the boiled veggies under cold water. Peel the potatoes. Cut the potatoes and carrot into small cubes. Add the peas, chopped pickles, mayo, mustard and salt and pepper to taste. Stir and adjust the salt. It can keep in the fridge for a few days. Serve it as a toast topping over baked sweet potato slices.

PER SERVING (4 SERVINGS): 487 Calories; 36 g Fat (53.9% calories from fat); 4.5 g Protein; 27 g Carbohydrate; 5 g Dietary Fiber; 0 mg Cholesterol; 498 mg Sodium

MASOOR DAL

I love the spices and vegan-friendly ingredients in Indian cuisine, and of course, the fact that most Indian dishes just feel like a warm, comforting hug. Lentils are an excellent way to get protein. They are also a powerhouse when it comes to fiber. Served with rice, greens and maybe a little gluten-free flatbread, this filling meal will hit the spot, guaranteed.

Serves 3

2 tbsp (30 ml) olive oil

½ onion, chopped

1 clove garlic, minced

1½ tsp (4 g) ground cumin

1 tsp (2 g) garam masala

½ tsp ground coriander

⅛ tsp cayenne pepper

½ red bell pepper, chopped

¼ cup (45 g) diced tomato

1 cup (200 g) dried red lentils

½ tsp grated fresh ginger

1 bay leaf

Salt

Zest and juice of ½ lemon

Serving Suggestions

Gluten-free flatbread (page 160)

Cooked white rice

Chopped parsley

Chopped green onions

Heat the olive oil in a saucepan over medium-high heat. Add the onion and garlic and cook until the onion starts becoming translucent, about 2 minutes. Add all the spices (do not add the ginger and bay leaf yet) and continue to cook for about a minute. Add the bell pepper and tomato and cook for another minute. Add 2½ cups (590 ml) of water and the lentils, ginger and bay leaf. Add salt to taste, lower the heat and let simmer for about 20 minutes. Turn off the heat, add the lemon zest and juice and stir. Optionally, serve alongside gluten-free flatbread, over white rice and garnished with chopped parsley and green onions.

PER SERVING (3 SERVINGS): 324 Calories; 10 g Fat (26.8% calories from fat); 19 g Protein; 43 g Carbohydrate; 21 g Dietary Fiber; 0 mg Cholesterol; 19 mg Sodium

BLACK BEAN ENCHILADAS

Loaded with black beans, these enchiladas are as powerful as they are delicious. The easy homemade enchilada sauce has just the right amount of spicy kick and that deeply satisfying umami flavor.

Serves 4

1 tbsp (15 ml) olive or coconut oil

1 medium red onion, finely chopped

2 cloves garlic, minced

1 tsp (2 g) red pepper flakes

2 tsp (5 g) ground cumin

1 medium jalapeño pepper, seeded and finely chopped

1 cup (250 g) tomato puree

2 tbsp (32 g) tomato paste

½ tsp dried thyme

Salt and freshly ground black pepper

1 bay leaf

1 (15-oz [425-g]) can black beans, drained and rinsed

10 to 12 (5½" [14 cm]) gluten-free corn tortillas

8 oz (240 g) vegan mozzarella cheese (optional)

2 tbsp (2 g) chopped fresh cilantro

Preheat the oven to 350°F (175°C). Heat the oil in a sauté pan over medium heat. Add the onion and garlic and cook for 3 minutes. Add the red pepper flakes and cumin and cook for another 2 minutes. Add the jalapeño, tomato puree, tomato paste, thyme, 1 cup (235 ml) of water, salt and pepper and stir well to combine. Add the bay leaf and black beans and bring to a boil. Lower the heat to low, mash the beans with a fork and let simmer for 5 minutes before turning off the heat.

Drain the bean mixture over a bowl and save the liquid as the enchilada sauce. Roll up the tortillas tightly with about 3 tablespoons (32 g) of the bean mixture in each tortilla. Spread half of the sauce on the bottom of a 9 x 13–inch (23 x 33–cm) baking dish and place the rolled-up tortillas in the dish, seam side down. Pour the remaining sauce over the tortillas. Sprinkle with the vegan cheese (if using), cover the baking dish with foil and bake for 15 minutes. Top with chopped cilantro before serving.

PER SERVING (4 SERVINGS): 823 Calories; 20 g Fat (21.3% calories from fat); 32 g Protein; 131 g Carbohydrate; 25 g Dietary Fiber; 0 mg Cholesterol; 1028 mg Sodium

PAD THAI

A fresh take on the Thai classic, this recipe incorporates a load of vegetables alongside a delicious sauce based on beans and peanut butter for a nutritional punch.

Serves 3

Peanut Sauce

½ (15-oz [425-g]) can white beans, drained and rinsed

½ cup (130 g) peanut butter (unsweetened)

1 tbsp (10 ml) apple cider vinegar

1 tbsp (15 ml) coconut aminos

1 tbsp (15 ml) pure maple syrup or agave nectar

4 tsp (11 g) grated fresh ginger

1 clove garlic, minced

¼ tsp red pepper flakes

Cooking Sauce

1 tbsp (15 ml) freshly squeezed lime juice

2 tbsp (30 ml) pure maple syrup or (24 g) coconut sugar

2 tbsp (30 ml) coconut aminos

Noodles

8 oz (227 g) Thai rice noodles

2 tbsp (30 ml) coconut oil

1 red onion, diced

2 cloves garlic, minced

¼ tsp red pepper flakes

1 carrot, julienne cut or diced

2 cups (142 g) broccoli florets

1 red bell pepper, julienne cut or diced

4 green onions, coarsely sliced

Optional Garnishes

Mung bean sprouts

Lime slices

To prepare the peanut sauce, combine all the peanut sauce ingredients with ¼ cup (60 ml) water in a food processor until smooth (add more water if too thick). Set aside. Next, prepare the cooking sauce. In a separate bowl, mix together the cooking sauce ingredients and set aside.

To prepare the noodles, cook the rice noodles according to the package directions, drain and set aside. Heat the coconut oil in a large sauté pan or wok over medium-high heat. Add the onion and cook for 4 minutes. Add the garlic and red pepper flakes and cook for another minute. Add the carrot, broccoli, red bell pepper and green onions and cook for 2 minutes. Finally, add the drained noodles together with the cooking sauce and cook for 2 more minutes. Serve with the peanut sauce, optionally topped with sprouts and lime.

PER SERVING (3 SERVINGS): 750 Calories; 26 g Fat (30.6% calories from fat); 17 g Protein; 118 g Carbohydrate; 10 g Dietary Fiber; 0 mg Cholesterol; 458 mg Sodium

RAMEN SOUP

Hearing the word *ramen* is enough to trigger cravings in me, every single time. It is just a delicious playground and it feels like a big, warm hug. The broth in this recipe is based on mushrooms and sunflower seeds, fortifying the deep umami taste with healthy fats and protein.

Serves 3

6 oz (170 g) gluten-free noodles (any kind you like)

Vegetables

1 tbsp (15 ml) sesame oil (or coconut oil or olive oil)

8 oz (227 g) mushrooms, sliced

3 cups (213 g) broccoli florets

Soup Base

1 tbsp (15 ml) sesame oil

½ medium onion, chopped

2 cloves garlic, sliced

¾ cup (109 g) roasted sunflower seeds

1 tbsp (15 ml) coconut aminos

1 tbsp (15 ml) cider vinegar

2 tbsp (30 ml) chili garlic sauce (or 1 tbsp [10 g] minced garlic and 1 tbsp [15 ml] chili oil)

2 tbsp (16 g) nutritional yeast

1 tbsp (15 g) tahini

4 cups (946 ml) mushroom stock

Salt and freshly ground black pepper

Optional Toppings

Green onions

Sprouts

Carrots

Radishes

Black sesame seeds

Sugar snap peas

Cook the noodles according to the package directions, drain and set aside. In a skillet over medium heat, heat the sesame oil, add the mushrooms and cook for 5 minutes. Add the broccoli florets and cook for another 3 minutes. Transfer the vegetable mixture to a bowl.

Prepare the soup base by adding the sesame oil to the same skillet used for the vegetables. Add the onion and garlic and cook for 4 minutes. Transfer the onion mixture to a blender along with the remaining soup base ingredients. Blend until smooth, transfer back to the skillet and bring to a boil. Combine the soup base, noodles and vegetable mixture in soup bowls and garnish with your choice of toppings.

PER SERVING (3 SERVINGS): 711 Calories; 43 g Fat (53.6% calories from fat); 20 g Protein; 64 g Carbohydrate; 9 g Dietary Fiber; 0 mg Cholesterol; 129 mg Sodium.

MOUSSAKA

Maybe it is not the most traditional definition of moussaka, but this simpler and healthier version has all the Mediterranean feels with layers of roasted eggplants and summer vegetables, along with chickpeas for added protein.

Serves 4

1 medium eggplant

¼ cup + 2 tbsp (90 ml) olive oil, divided

1 shallot or onion, chopped

2 cloves garlic, minced

1 red bell pepper, chopped

1 green bell pepper, chopped

2 tomatoes, chopped

2 tbsp (32 g) tomato paste

1 (15-oz [425-g]) can chickpeas, drained and rinsed

¼ tsp dried thyme (optional)

¼ tsp dried oregano (optional)

Salt and freshly ground black pepper

Preheat the oven to 400°F (200°C). Slice the eggplants into approximately ½-inch (1.3-cm)-thick circles. Brush the eggplants with ¼ cup (60 ml) of the olive oil and roast them in the oven for 25 minutes.

Heat the remaining 2 tablespoons (30 ml) of olive oil in a large skillet over medium-high heat, add the shallot and cook, stirring, for 1 minute. Add the garlic and bell peppers and cook for 2 minutes. Add the tomatoes, tomato paste, ¼ cup (60 ml) of water and the chickpeas. Add the thyme and oregano (if using), and salt and black pepper to taste. Cook, stirring, for another 5 minutes. In the bottom of another large skillet (I used cast iron for this), arrange one layer of roasted eggplant. Cover with the sautéed vegetables. Place another layer of eggplant on top and repeat until you fill the pan, ending with a layer of eggplant. Cook for 10 minutes over medium-low heat.

PER SERVING (4 SERVINGS): 639 Calories; 27 g Fat (27.7% calories from fat); 23 g Protein; 81 g Carbohydrate; 24 g Dietary Fiber; 0 mg Cholesterol; 103 mg Sodium

PINEAPPLE FRIED RICE

Rice and peas are a potent combination to support fitness goals. Quick and easy, this recipe sweetens the deal further with pineapples.

Serves 3

1 cup (195 g) uncooked rice (or use 2½ cups [328 g] leftover cooked rice)

2 tbsp (30 ml) coconut oil or olive oil

½ red onion, diced

1 tbsp (8 g) grated fresh ginger

1 tsp (4 g) coconut sugar

2 tbsp (30 ml) coconut aminos

1 cup (165 g) pineapple chunks

1 red bell pepper, diced

¾ cup (105 g) frozen or fresh corn

¾ cup (113 g) peas

3 green onions, chopped

Cook the rice according to the package directions. Heat the coconut oil in a large skillet over medium-high heat. Add the onion and ginger and cook, stirring often, for 3 minutes. Add the sugar and coconut aminos and mix well. Add the pineapple chunks, bell pepper, corn and peas and cook for 3 more minutes. Top with the green onions before serving.

PER SERVING (3 SERVINGS): 427 Calories; 10 g Fat (21.4% calories from fat); 8 g Protein; 77 g Carbohydrate; 5 g Dietary Fiber; 0 mg Cholesterol; 191 mg Sodium

SUPER COMBO SUSHI

Rolled around avocado-pea-mint mash, homemade vegan kimchi, massaged purple cabbage and sprouts, these are a mouthful in size, sheer deliciousness and nutrition with a balanced combination of protein, carbs, healthy fats and probiotics.

Serves 3

Avocado-Pea-Mint Mash

¾ cup (98 g) frozen (defrosted) or fresh peas

1 clove garlic, minced

Juice of ½ lemon

Salt and freshly ground black pepper

¼ cup (24 g) chopped fresh mint leaves

1 medium avocado

2 green onions, finely chopped

1 tsp (5 ml) olive oil

¼ cup (36 g) roasted unsalted sunflower seeds

Red Cabbage Salad

¾ cup (255 g) finely sliced red cabbage

1 tbsp (15 ml) freshly squeezed lemon juice

¼ tsp salt

¼ tsp olive oil

Sushi

1 cup (128 g) cooked white sticky rice

2 nori sheets

½ cup (125 g) Kimchi (page 174)

½ cup (50 g) bean sprouts

1 tsp (3 g) black sesame seeds (optional)

Prepare the avocado-pea-mint mash by combining the peas with the garlic, lemon juice and salt and pepper to taste in a large bowl. Mash the peas with a fork, add the mint, avocado, green onions and olive oil, and mash again to combine. Finally, add the sunflower seeds, mix well and set aside.

In a bowl, combine the red cabbage salad ingredients and massage with your fingers to mix and soften.

To roll the sushi, you can use a thick towel spread over a flat surface. Cut some plastic wrap to spread over the towel and place a nori sheet on the plastic wrap. Spread half of the rice over the nori sheet, working with your fingertips and covering the entire surface of the nori sheet. Add half of the avocado pea mint mash, red cabbage salad, kimchi and the sprouts on one side of each nori sheet, taking up about a third of it. Start rolling the nori sheet along with towel and the wrap, peeling off the towel and the wrap as they get in the way. Keep rolling with your hands and cut the roll into 4 pieces. Repeat with another sheet of nori. Sprinkle the cut sides of the sushi rolls with black sesame seeds (if using).

PER SERVING (3 SERVINGS): 230 Calories; 9 g Fat (32.8% calories from fat); 9 g Protein; 31 g Carbohydrate; 5 g Dietary Fiber; 0 mg Cholesterol; 373 mg Sodium

TIKKA DAL

It is amazing how magical the combination of a few spices can be. The high-protein duo of lentils and quinoa is brought alive in a wonderful tikka sauce, delivering nutrition, comfort and sweet heat.

Serves 3

½ cup (87 g) uncooked quinoa

½ cup (100 g) dried green lentils

Salt

2 tbsp (30 ml) coconut oil

1 large white onion, finely chopped

2 tsp (5 g) ground cumin

1 tsp (2 g) ground coriander

¼ tsp ground cardamom

¼ tsp ground nutmeg

¼ tsp paprika

¼ tsp cayenne pepper

1 clove garlic, minced

1 tbsp (8 g) grated fresh ginger

½ cup (90 g) diced tomato

2 tbsp (32 g) tomato paste

1 cup (235 ml) coconut cream or coconut milk

2 handfuls of stemmed and chopped kale

Serving Suggestions

Gluten-free flatbread (page 160)

Cucumber slices

Purple carrot slices

Lime slices

Fresh cilantro

Rinse the quinoa and lentils, then place them in a pot with a pinch of salt and 4 cups (946 ml) of water. Bring to a boil, lower the heat and let simmer for 20 minutes. Drain and set aside.

Heat the coconut oil in a large skillet over medium-high heat. Add the onion and spices and cook, stirring, for 2 minutes. Add the garlic and ginger and cook for another 3 minutes. Add the tomato and tomato paste and mix well. Add the coconut cream and stir. Add salt as needed and cook for 1 more minute. Finally, add the cooked quinoa mixture along with the kale and cook for another minute. Serve hot, optionally along with the listed serving suggestions.

PER SERVING (3 SERVINGS): 550 Calories; 40 g Fat (61.0% calories from fat); 13 g Protein; 45 g Carbohydrate; 8 g Dietary Fiber; 0 mg Cholesterol; 132 mg Sodium

VEGETABLES WITH PEANUT CURRY

This simple Thai-inspired curry has an amazingly creamy and flavorful sauce accompanying and transforming a large portion of vegetables into a satisfying meal.

Serves 3

Peanut Curry Sauce

3 tbsp (48 g) peanut butter

1½ tsp (4 g) curry powder

1 tsp (5 ml) pure maple syrup

1 tbsp (15 ml) coconut aminos

Juice of ½ lime

⅛ tsp cayenne pepper (optional)

1 clove garlic, minced

1½ tsp (4 g) grated fresh ginger

Vegetables

2 tbsp (30 ml) coconut oil (or other cooking oil)

1 small onion, thinly sliced

1 bell pepper, julienne cut

1 carrot, chopped or sliced

2 stalks celery, thinly sliced

In a bowl, combine all the peanut curry sauce ingredients along with ¼ cup (60 ml) of water (use more water if still too thick), mix well and set aside. Heat the oil in a wok or large skillet over medium-high heat, add all the vegetables and cook, stirring, for 5 minutes. Plate the vegetables and serve with the peanut curry sauce.

PER SERVING (3 SERVINGS): 249 Calories; 18 g Fat (59.4% calories from fat); 6 g Protein; 21 g Carbohydrate; 5 g Dietary Fiber; 0 mg Cholesterol; 203 mg Sodium

SWEET-AND-SOUR CAULIFLOWER

The signature Asian sweet-and-sour mouthwatering taste you came to love flavors a healthy combination of cauliflower and chickpeas in this simple recipe.

Serves 3

1 medium cauliflower, cut into florets

3 tbsp (45 ml) vegetable oil

⅓ cup (43 g) arrowroot starch or cornstarch

1 (15-oz [425-g]) can chickpeas, drained and rinsed

Sauce

½ cup (100 g) sugar

½ cup (120 ml) apple cider vinegar

2 tbsp (30 ml) coconut aminos

1 tsp (3 g) garlic powder

½ tsp onion powder

¼ cup (60 g) ketchup

1 tbsp (8 g) arrowroot starch or cornstarch

Serving Suggestions

Cooked white rice

Sliced radish

Chopped green onion

Arugula

Toasted sesame seeds

Preheat the oven to 400°F (200°C). In a large bowl. combine the cauliflower florets with the oil and mix. Add the starch and toss until uniformly coated. Transfer to a baking dish and roast in the oven for 15 minutes. Add the chickpeas, stir and roast for another 5 minutes. In a medium bowl, combine the sauce ingredients, making sure the sugar fully dissolves. Pour the sauce over the cauliflower, stir to coat and roast for 2 more minutes. Optionally serve over rice with the suggested garnishes.

PER SERVING (3 SERVINGS): 935 Calories; 23 g Fat (21.3% calories from fat); 33 g Protein; 158 g Carbohydrate; 31 g Dietary Fiber; 0 mg Cholesterol; 510 mg Sodium

CARAMEL CANDY BARS

I have achieved true vegan caramel bliss with this recipe. From taste to texture, I love everything about it. The caramel itself is based on almond butter, coconut oil and maple syrup, so it is simple and wholesome. The base is made with coconut flour and is nutritious, crunchy and delicious. It is essentially a candy bar, only as healthy as they come.

Serves 6

Crust

¾ cup (84 g) coconut flour

⅓ cup (67 g) coconut sugar

⅓ cup (80 ml) coconut oil

1 tbsp (15 ml) pure vanilla extract

¼ tsp ground cinnamon

Caramel Sauce

⅓ cup (80 ml) coconut oil

⅓ cup (87 g) almond butter

½ cup (120 ml) pure maple syrup

1 tbsp (15 ml) pure vanilla extract

¼ tsp sea salt

Chocolate Coating

⅔ cup (160 ml) coconut oil, melted

⅔ cup (74 g) unsweetened cocoa powder

⅓ cup (80 ml) pure maple syrup

Pinch of salt

Preheat the oven to 350°F (175°C). In a large bowl, combine the crust ingredients and mix well. Line a baking dish (5 x 7 inches [12.5 x 18 cm]) with parchment paper and spread the crust mixture evenly in the dish. Bake for 25 minutes, remove from the oven and let cool.

In a saucepan, combine the caramel sauce ingredients and cook, stirring, over medium-high heat for 5 minutes. Remove from the heat, let cool and spread the caramel sauce over the cooled baked crust. Chill in the freezer for at least 10 minutes while you prepare the chocolate coating.

In a medium bowl, combine all the chocolate coating ingredients. Set a wire rack over a baking sheet. Take the filled crust out of the freezer and cut into candy bar–size bits to your liking. Place the bits on the rack and pour the chocolate coating over them, making sure they are fully coated. Keep the candy bars in the freezer and thaw for 5 minutes before serving.

PER SERVING (6 SERVINGS): 630 Calories; 47 g Fat (64.9% calories from fat); 5 g Protein; 53 g Carbohydrate; 7 g Dietary Fiber; 0 mg Cholesterol; 95 mg Sodium

PEANUT BUTTER CHOCOLATE FUDGE BITES

Keep these bite-sized, power-packed, delightful chocolate treats at the ready for when the dessert craving hits. This is extremely easy to make, with a short ingredient list and no cooking involved. And it is well proven to be a great party pleaser.

Serves 4

1 cup (260 g) peanut butter

4 oz (55 g) vegan dark chocolate, melted

¼ cup (34 g) roasted hazelnuts

⅓ cup (60 ml) pure maple syrup

¼ cup (60 ml) almond milk

1 tsp (5 ml) pure vanilla extract

Pinch of salt

Topping
¼ cup (34 g) roasted hazelnuts, coarsely chopped

In a food processor, combine all the ingredients, except the topping, and process until smooth. Line a container (approximately 5 x 7 inches [12.5 x 18 cm]) with parchment paper and spread the mixture in the container. Sprinkle with the topping, cover and refrigerate overnight (or chill for at least 2 hours in the freezer). Serve frozen or thawed, depending on your preference.

PER SERVING (4 SERVINGS): 680 Calories; 52 g Fat (47.6% calories from fat); 19 g Protein; 47 g Carbohydrate; 6 g Dietary Fiber; 0 mg Cholesterol; 339 mg Sodium

MATCHA BARS WITH CACAO NIBS

I often find myself having a nice dessert for breakfast simply because, why not? Once you are in the realm of delicious, fulfilling and perfectly nutritious desserts, there is no going back.

What makes this one special, of course, is the matcha (green tea powder). Matcha is considered a powerful superfood and a great source of antioxidants.

Serves 4

Crust
½ cup (68 g) roasted hazelnuts

¾ cup (110 g) raisins

Pinch of salt

Filling
1 tsp (2 g) matcha powder

½ cup (120 ml) almond milk

1 cup (140 g) raw cashews

2 tbsp to ¼ cup (30 to 60 ml) pure maple syrup

2 tbsp (30 ml) freshly squeezed lemon juice

¼ cup (30 g) cacao nibs

Optional Topping
2 oz (55 g) vegan dark chocolate, melted

In a food processor, combine all the crust ingredients and process until it starts to get a sticky consistency but doesn't turn into a dough; make sure to leave some texture. Line a cake pan or container (approximately 5 x 7 inches [12.5 x 18 cm]) with parchment paper and spread the crust mixture on the bottom. Place the pan in the freezer to chill while you prepare the filling.

In a high-speed blender, combine all the filling ingredients, except the cacao nibs, and blend them until smooth. Stir in the cacao nibs with a spoon and spread the filling over the crust. Refrigerate overnight or for at least 4 hours. I decorated mine by drizzling it with melted dark chocolate. Be careful not to heat the chocolate too much, though, to avoid melting the filling.

PER SERVING (4 SERVINGS): 565 Calories, 39 g Fat (56.6% calories from fat); 11 g Protein; 55 g Carbohydrate; 6 g Dietary Fiber; 0 mg Cholesterol; 44 mg Sodium

STRAWBERRY-TOPPED CHEESECAKE

Vegan cheesecakes are easy to make despite how sophisticated and luscious they look and taste. And they are everyone's favorite when it comes to dessert time. Mostly nut based, this cheesecake manages to sneak in some protein and healthy fats when you think you are being naughty.

Serves 6

Crust

1½ cups (150 g) pecans

¾ cup (110 g) raisins

Pinch of salt

1 tsp (50 ml) pure vanilla extract

Cream Layer

2 cups (280 g) raw cashews (preferably soaked in water overnight or for at least 4 hours)

1 (14-oz [397-g]) can coconut cream

Juice of 1 lemon

½ cup (120 ml) pure maple syrup

1 tsp (5 ml) pure vanilla extract

Top Layer

2 cups (510 g) frozen strawberries

A few fresh strawberries, hulled and sliced

In a food processor, combine the crust ingredients and process until you get a sticky paste. Between 2 sheets of parchment paper, roll out the crust to fit your pan or mold (I used a 6-inch [15-cm]-diameter mold) that has a release feature. If your pan doesn't have a release, I suggest lining the pan with parchment paper first. Lay the crust on the bottom of the pan and place it in the freezer.

In a high-speed blender, combine all the cream layer ingredients and blend until smooth. Pour the cream mixture over the crust, spread uniformly and place back in the freezer. Process the frozen strawberries in the cleaned food processor, spread over the cream layer and chill in the freezer for a few hours or overnight. Thaw for 10 minutes or more at room temperature and top with fresh strawberry slices before serving.

PER SERVING (6 SERVINGS): 875 Calories; 65 g Fat (62.5% calories from fat); 15 g Protein; 73 g Carbohydrate; 7 g Dietary Fiber; 0 mg Cholesterol; 37 mg Sodium

ALMOND BUTTER CHOCOLATE BROWNIES

This luscious, rich and fudgy brownie has a great form and texture while keeping it all wholesome and nutritious. The almond butter, nuts and oat flour all contribute as protein components, among the other nutrients and fiber they introduce into this recipe.

Serves 6

Brownies

⅓ cup (80 ml) coconut oil, melted, plus more to grease pan (optional)

2 tbsp (14 g) flaxseed meal

⅓ cup (87 g) natural, unsalted almond butter

½ cup (100 g) coconut sugar

½ cup (120 ml) pure maple syrup

¾ cup (83 g) unsweetened cocoa powder

1 tsp (5 ml) pure vanilla extract

¼ tsp salt

⅓ cup (34 g) gluten-free oat flour

½ cup (55 g) chopped pecans

¼ cup (44 g) vegan dark chocolate chips

Topping

¼ cup (60 ml) coconut oil, melted

2 tbsp (30 ml) pure maple syrup

3 Medjool dates, pitted

¼ tsp salt

Preheat the oven to 325°F (160°C). Line an 8-inch (20.5-cm) square baking pan with parchment paper or coconut oil–greased foil and set aside.

In a small bowl, whisk the flaxseed meal with 6 tablespoons (90 ml) of water and set aside for 5 minutes to thicken into flax eggs. In a medium bowl, thoroughly mix the almond butter, coconut sugar, maple syrup and ⅓ cup (80 ml) of coconut oil. Add the cocoa powder, vanilla and salt and whisk more until thoroughly combined. Add the flax eggs and whisk everything together. Finally, add the oat flour and stir it in with a rubber spatula. Fold in the pecans and chocolate chips and pour the batter evenly into the pan. Bake for 25 to 30 minutes. Remove from the oven and let cool for 1 hour.

In a food processor, combine the topping ingredients and process, then drizzle over the baked brownies.

PER SERVING (6 SERVINGS): 629 Calories; 41 g Fat (36.4% calories from fat); 6 g Protein; 72 g Carbohydrate; 6 g Dietary Fiber; 0 mg Cholesterol; 185 mg Sodium

CARAMEL TART

It is dessert time—and time to impress yourself and anyone else with this sophisticated, luscious tart. Just don't tell anyone how easy it was to make. The recipe involves running a few groups of ingredients through the food processor and layering them. No baking, no tricks, and an amazing treat that features healthy fats and minimal use of wholesome sweets.

Serves 6

Crust

1½ cups (150 g) pecans

¾ cup (136 g) pitted Medjool dates

Pinch of salt

Caramel Layer

1 cup (178 g) pitted Medjool dates

½ cup (70 g) raw cashews (preferably soaked in water for at least 4 hours)

½ cup (120 ml) coconut cream

¼ tsp salt

1 tbsp (15 ml) pure maple syrup

Chocolate Topping

2 tbsp (14 g) unsweetened cocoa powder

2 tbsp (30 ml) coconut oil, melted

2 tbsp (30 ml) pure maple syrup

1 tsp (5 ml) pure vanilla extract

Optional Decorations

Cacao nibs

Coconut chips

Berries

In a food processor, combine the crust ingredients and process until you get a sticky paste. Between 2 sheets of parchment paper, roll out the crust to fit your pan or mold (I used a 6-inch [15-cm]-diameter mold) that has a release feature. If your pan doesn't have a release, I suggest lining the pan with parchment paper first. Lay the crust on the bottom of the pan and chill it in the freezer while you work on the filling. In a high-speed blender, combine all the caramel layer ingredients and blend until smooth. Spread this mixture over the chilled crust and place back in the freezer.

In a small bowl, stir together all the chocolate topping ingredients and pour over the caramel layer. Decorate the tart with the toppings (if using) and chill in the freezer overnight or for at least a few hours. It can be served right out of the freezer (it will still come out relatively soft), or thawed slightly before serving.

PER SERVING (6 SERVINGS): 534 Calories; 36 g Fat (56.3% calories from fat); 7 g Protein; 57 g Carbohydrate; 7 g Dietary Fiber; 0 mg Cholesterol; 116 mg Sodium

PEANUT BUTTER CHOCOLATE DONUT HOLES

These perfect little energizing treats pack a lot in taste and fall season feelings besides being a good source of protein and fiber. This is another good option to have at the ready and keep in the freezer, although it wouldn't be a big deal to make this easy recipe on a whim, either.

Serves 4

Donut Holes

1 cup (80 g) gluten-free rolled oats

½ cup (130 g) peanut butter

1½ cups (218 g) raisins

¼ cup (28 g) unsweetened cocoa powder

2 tbsp (30 ml) coconut oil

2 tsp (5 g) ground cinnamon

1 tsp (3 g) grated fresh ginger (optional)

Glaze

2 tbsp (30 ml) coconut oil, melted

2 tbsp (15 g) powdered sugar

1 tsp (5 ml) pure vanilla extract or (5 g) vanilla bean powder

In a food processor, combine the donut hole ingredients and process until you get a sticky dough. Shape into bite-size balls and chill in the freezer for at least 20 minutes before applying the glaze.

To make the glaze, in a bowl, stir together the melted coconut oil, powdered sugar and vanilla until smooth. Dip the donut holes into the glaze before serving.

PER SERVING (4 SERVINGS): 479 Calories; 32 g Fat (57.0% calories from fat); 12 g Protein; 42 g Carbohydrate; 6 g Dietary Fiber; 0 mg Cholesterol; 153 mg Sodium

PISTACHIO RICE CHOCOLATE BARS

These bars have a lot of texture play alongside chocolaty deliciousness, another great treat option to keep ready for quick pick-me-ups and fuel-ups. It takes no time to prepare: Just combine the ingredients and put in the freezer. No cooking, no baking whatsoever.

Serves 4

½ cup (120 ml) coconut oil, melted

2 tbsp (32 g) peanut butter

¼ cup (60 ml) pure maple syrup

1 tsp (5 ml) pure vanilla extract

¼ cup (28 g) unsweetened cocoa powder

Pinch of salt

½ cup (62 g) chopped pistachios

¾ cup (16 g) gluten-free crispy rice cereal

Line a baking dish or a container (approximately 5 x 7 inches [12.5 x 18 cm]) with parchment paper. In a large bowl, combine the melted coconut oil and peanut butter and mix well. Add the maple syrup, vanilla, cocoa powder and salt and mix again. Finally, stir in the pistachios and rice cereal. Pour the mixture into the lined container. Cover and keep in the freezer for at least 4 hours before serving.

PER SERVING (4 SERVINGS): 484 Calories; 43 g Fat (75.4% calories from fat); 5 g Protein; 27 g Carbohydrate; 4 g Dietary Fiber; 0 mg Cholesterol; 135 mg Sodium

SNACKS
& BASICS

An active lifestyle is also one where time is in short supply and sitting down for a meal is not always a possibility, and you just need a worthy snack to fuel up on pre- or post-workout. This chapter offers a mix of quick-make options, items you can prep ahead and take on the go, and some basics to keep at the ready so that you can improvise.

FOUR-SEED GRANOLA BARS

A vegan protein bar that is gluten-free, nut-free and soy-free with no refined sugars. Made with oats, three seeds and other plant magic, this is so deliciously chewy and tasty, as tested by the house folk and the neighbors. All in all, I think these lasted about fifteen minutes before disappearing without a trace.

Serves 4

1½ cups (120 g) gluten-free rolled oats

⅓ cup (48 g) sesame seeds

2 tbsp (20 g) chia seeds

2 tbsp (18 g) sunflower seeds

2 tbsp (14 g) flaxseeds, ground or whole

⅓ cup (80 g) tahini

1 cup (145 g) raisins

2 tbsp (30 ml) pure maple syrup or agave nectar

Optional Topping

Melted vegan dark chocolate

Preheat the oven to 350°F (175°C). On a dry baking sheet, oven-roast the oats and sesame seeds for 15 minutes. Transfer to a bowl, add the chia, sunflower and flaxseeds, stir and set aside. The tahini should be a little runny. If it is too thick, mix it with water to thin. In a food processor, combine the tahini, raisins and maple syrup and process until you get a sticky paste. Add the paste to the seed mixture and mix thoroughly.

Line a baking dish or a rectangular container (I used a 5 x 7-inch [12.5 x 18–cm] dish) with plastic wrap or parchment paper. Transfer the mix to the lined dish and press with your fingers to shape into an even layer. Cover the dish and refrigerate or freeze for 20 minutes. Cut into slices and drizzle with melted chocolate (if using).

PER SERVING (4 SERVINGS): 513 Calories; 24 g Fat (40.8% calories from fat); 15 g Protein; 65 g Carbohydrate; 10 g Dietary Fiber; 0 mg Cholesterol; 32 mg Sodium

OVERNIGHT CHOCOLATE COFFEE CHIA PUDDING

Chia seed puddings can be excellent options for starting the day right with a good portion of complete proteins and omega-3s. And I also wouldn't mind a chocolate coffee–flavored delicious dessert or post-workout snack. The recipe is as simple as putting the ingredients together and waiting for morning.

Serves 2

1 cup (235 ml) almond milk

½ cup (120 ml) brewed coffee

3 tbsp (21 g) unsweetened cocoa powder

3 tbsp (45 ml) pure maple syrup

1 tsp (5 ml) pure vanilla extract

Pinch of salt

⅓ cup (53 g) chia seeds

Optional Toppings

Coconut cream

Fruits

In a large bowl, combine all the ingredients, except the chia seeds and toppings, and stir. Add the chia seeds last and stir again. Split between 2 serving cups, add your favorite toppings and let chill in the fridge overnight.

PER SERVING (2 SERVINGS): 297 Calories; 13 g Fat (38.2% calories from fat); 5 g Protein; 43 g Carbohydrate; 3 g Dietary Fiber; 0 mg Cholesterol; 93 mg Sodium

TURMERIC GINGER SMOOTHIE

Get your fruit portions of the day, energize and boost your immune system in one delicious drink with this potent super-smoothie.

Serves 1

½ cup (93 g) frozen pineapple

½ cup (83 g) frozen mango

1 banana, preferably frozen

1 tsp (3 g) grated fresh ginger

1 tsp (3 g) grated fresh turmeric

1 scoop (30 g) vegan protein powder (optional)

Serving Suggestion

Mixed berries

In a high-speed blender, combine all the ingredients along with 1½ cups (355 ml) of water and blend. Serve in a glass, optionally topped with berries.

> **PER TOTAL RECIPE:** 207 Calories; 1 g Fat (5.2% calories from fat); 2 g Protein; 52 g Carbohydrate; 6 g Dietary Fiber; 0 mg Cholesterol; 8 mg Sodium

QUINOA AVOCADO BREAD

Wholesome, firm and earthy, this magical protein-dense bread is made of quinoa, almonds and avocado so that you can feel great about eating a sandwich. It is also delicious on its own, for toast or as a side to soups.

Serves 4

2 tbsp (14 g) flaxseed meal

2½ cups (313 g) quinoa flour

2 cups (190 g) almond meal

1 tsp (5 g) baking powder

Pinch of salt

Zest and juice of 1 lime

1 avocado, peeled, pitted and mashed

1 tbsp (15 ml) pure maple syrup

Preheat the oven to 350°F (175°C). In a small bowl, stir the flaxseed meal with ⅓ cup (80 ml) of water to make a flax egg and set aside. In a large bowl, mix together the quinoa flour, almond meal, baking powder and salt. In a separate small bowl, stir together the lime zest and juice, mashed avocado and maple syrup. Combine with the quinoa mixture along with the flax egg and an additional ½ cup (120 ml) of water and knead into a dough. Slowly add more water if the dough is too dry.

Split the dough into 4 equal portions, shape each into a ball and flatten them slightly. Place the dough balls on a baking sheet lined with parchment paper and bake for 20 to 25 minutes. Test whether they are done by poking a toothpick in the center; it should come out clean. Remove from the oven and let cool completely before serving.

PER SERVING (4 SERVINGS): 195 Calories; 6 g Fat (26.5% calories from fat); 8 g Protein; 28 g Carbohydrate; 4 g Dietary Fiber; 0 mg Cholesterol; 449 mg Sodium

FLATBREAD

I am a big fan of flatbreads, but not so much a fan of the nutritional guilt bread comes with. Made with quinoa and garbanzo bean flours, this seasoned flatbread is incredibly tasty besides being a dense source of protein. Enjoy it to your heart's content and feel good about it.

Serves 6

2 tbsp (14 g) flaxseed meal

1 cup (125 g) quinoa flour

1 cup (125 g) garbanzo bean flour, plus more for dusting

1 tsp (5 g) baking powder

1 tsp (6 g) salt

¼ tsp ground cumin

¼ tsp dried thyme

¼ tsp onion powder

1 tbsp (15 ml) olive oil

Cooking oil for panfrying

In a small bowl, stir the flaxseed meal with ⅓ cup (80 ml) of water to make a flax egg and set aside. In a large bowl, combine the rest of the ingredients except the cooking oil, add the flax egg and an additional ½ cup (120 ml) of water and knead into dough. Slowly add more water if it is too dry.

Split the dough into 6 equal portions and shape each into a ball. Dust a clean surface with garbanzo bean flour and use a rolling pin to roll each dough ball into approximately 6-inch (15-cm)-diameter circles. Heat the cooking oil in a medium skillet over medium-high heat. When the oil is hot, place a dough disk in the pan and cook for a few minutes on each side, until you get golden brown crust spots. Repeat with the rest of the dough.

PER SERVING (6 SERVINGS): 195 Calories; 6 g Fat (26.5% calories from fat); 8 g Protein; 28 g Carbohydrate; 4 g Dietary Fiber; 0 mg Cholesterol; 449 mg Sodium

BASIL CREAM CHEESE

Making your own basic plant-based cheese is extremely easy and rewarding. Here is a variation that is mildly spiced up, and brightened with basil. Healthy, creamy and flavorful, this cheese will go great in sandwiches, as a spread over toast, as a dip or as a sauce component over pasta. It will keep in the fridge for up to a week.

Makes 1½ cups (360 g) cream cheese

1½ cups (210 g) raw cashews (preferably soaked in water for 4 hours, then drained)

½ cup (120 ml) coconut cream

½ tsp onion powder

½ tsp garlic powder

¼ tsp freshly ground black pepper

3 tbsp (24 g) nutritional yeast

1 tbsp (16 g) chickpea miso

Pinch of ground nutmeg

Juice of ½ lemon

¼ tsp cayenne pepper

¼ tsp sea salt

⅓ cup (13 g) tightly packed fresh basil

Serving Suggestions

Gluten-free bagels

Sprouts

In a high-speed blender, combine all the ingredients with ½ cup (120 ml) of water and blend until creamy. Transfer to a container and keep the cheese on the countertop, covered, for 1 to 2 hours for a more fermented taste. Refrigerate overnight before serving.

PER SERVING (6 SERVINGS): 308 Calories; 25 g Fat (11.3% calories from fat); 10 g Protein; 16 g Carbohydrate; 3 g Dietary Fiber; 0 mg Cholesterol; 192 mg Sodium

BROCCOLI PESTO

Broccoli clearly deserves its reputation as being among the healthiest vegetables. But for all that fame, the fact that it packs a good deal of protein is often overlooked! This recipe is one of my favorite ways to get a lot of broccoli in. It takes little time to make, will store in the fridge and will give you a beautifully fresh and zesty sauce to transform your pasta. It is also perfectly yummy on toast or as a dip.

Makes 2 cups (495 g)

4 cups (284 g) broccoli florets

¾ cup (105 g) raw cashews

1 tbsp (15 ml) lemon juice

2 cloves garlic

2 tbsp (16 g) nutritional yeast

1 cup (40 g) tightly packed fresh basil or (96 g) mint leaves

1 tsp (1 g) red pepper flakes

3 tbsp (45 ml) olive oil

Salt and freshly ground black pepper

Steam or boil the broccoli florets for 3 to 5 minutes. In a food processor, combine the cashews, lemon juice, garlic and nutritional yeast and process them well. Add the broccoli, basil leaves, red pepper flakes, olive oil and salt and black pepper to taste, and process them again until everything is well combined, leaving a moderate texture. Serve with pasta mixed with roasted peppers, tomatoes and pine nuts or as a dip.

PER SERVING (6 SERVINGS): 196 Calories; 16 g Fat (11.3% calories from fat); 6 g Protein; 10 g Carbohydrate; 3 g Dietary Fiber; 0 mg Cholesterol; 18 mg Sodium

ROASTED EGGPLANT HUMMUS

The super dip called hummus has a lot going for it already. Of course, it is addictively delicious, while being nutritious and a good source of protein. But what is already perfect can be made even better if you add that wonderfully smoky flavor of roasted eggplant.

Makes 2 cups (495 g)

1 medium eggplant

1 (15-oz [425-g]) can chickpeas, drained and rinsed

¼ cup (60 ml) freshly squeezed lemon juice

2 cloves garlic, crushed

1 tbsp (15 ml) olive oil

2 tbsp (30 g) tahini

½ tsp salt

½ tsp freshly ground black pepper

½ tsp ground cumin

Roast the eggplant directly over a burner on the stovetop over medium heat, turning occasionally until it is fully soft and mushy, about 15 minutes. The eggplant is best cooked over an open flame, where it will develop its signature smoky flavor. If you don't have a gas stove, you can use a grill or roast directly over the cooking surface of an electric stove. Let the roasted eggplant cool and peel away the skin. In a food processor or high-speed blender, combine the roasted eggplant and all the remaining ingredients along with ¼ cup (60 ml) of water. Mix until smooth.

PER SERVING (6 SERVINGS): 312 Calories; 9 g Fat (4.1% calories from fat); 15 g Protein; 45 g Carbohydrate; 13 g Dietary Fiber; 0 mg Cholesterol; 201 mg Sodium

NACHO CHEESE SAUCE

Nachos are a lot of fun to play with. You get to spread your favorite proteins and vegetables within layers of corn chips. It is a great way to fuel up when you need to, especially when you have a vegetable-based, healthy and convincing cheesy sauce like this. Feel free to use the sauce for non-nacho purposes; it will function very well as a dip or pasta sauce.

Makes 2 cups (495 g)

6 medium potatoes, peeled and cubed

1 carrot, chopped

¼ cup (60 ml) olive oil

¼ cup (60 ml) plant-based milk

Juice of ½ lemon

2 tbsp (16 g) nutritional yeast

1½ tsp (17 g) Dijon mustard

½ tsp garlic powder

½ tsp onion powder

½ tsp smoked paprika

In a medium saucepan, combine the potatoes and carrot and add water to cover. Bring to a boil, lower the heat and let simmer, covered, for 20 minutes. Drain the water and transfer the potatoes and carrots to a food processor along with the rest of the ingredients. Process until totally smooth and serve warm.

PER SERVING (4 SERVINGS): 292 Calories; 14 g Fat (10.6% calories from fat); 7 g Protein; 31 g Carbohydrate; 5 g Dietary Fiber; 0 mg Cholesterol; 43 mg Sodium

PROBIOTICS

Your body is teeming with bacteria, both good and bad. Probiotics are the good guys that help with absorbing nutrients and keeping your gut healthy. Many fermented foods are considered probiotics, and besides their health benefits, the amazing sour treats presented in this chapter are worth keeping in your fridge just on the merit of their deliciousness.

Please note, most raw vegetables can be safely fermented at home if it is done correctly. In fact, fermented foods are often considered safer than raw vegetables since the naturally occurring lactic acid kills harmful bacteria. However, I encourage you to read food safety basics for fermentation, a quick web search will get you there. For good measure, I will summarize a few important points: Start with clean raw vegetables that are as fresh as possible. Thoroughly wash all the produce you will be using, any utensils, containers, surfaces and your hands. Another safety concern is contamination after fermenting. If you want to preserve your fermented foods, avoid things like eating (or drinking) directly out of the jar (I know the temptation). Transfer the portion you are going to consume into a new container with a clean utensil.

NOTE: Nutrition facts for fermented food are tricky because the sugar is consumed by bacteria. For that reason, they are not provided for the recipes in this chapter.

HOME-BREWED KOMBUCHA

I am a huge fan of kombucha. It is my favorite drink by far, not only for its amazing health benefits and probiotic properties, but for its mildly sour and refreshing taste. Get the biggest benefit of this superdrink by home brewing it. As a bonus, you get to flavor your drink with your favorite fruits, herbs or ginger for a zestier option.

Makes 100 oz (3 L)

13 cups (3.1 L) filtered water, divided

1 tbsp (6 g) loose-leaf black tea

1 tbsp (6 g) loose-leaf green tea

1 cup (100 g) coconut sugar (or any sugar)

1 cup (235 ml) starter kombucha from previous batch or store-bought kombucha

1 kombucha scoby

To start, you first need to brew tea. You can brew directly in a 2-gallon (7.6-L) jar or use a smaller glass container for ease. Bring 4 cups (946 L) of the filtered water to a boil and pour it into the jar. Use a tea strainer to steep the tea leaves in the boiling water for 10 minutes. Add the sugar, stir well with the wooden spoon until the sugar is dissolved and add the remaining 9 cups (2.1 L) of cold filtered water. Add the starter kombucha and the scoby. Stretch a piece of cloth over the opening of the jar and secure with a rubber band. Keep the jar in a dark place to ferment for 7 to 10 days. Depending on temperature, the fermenting time will vary. The hotter it is, the quicker the fermentation. The kombucha will get more sour and vinegary with more fermentation. You can start taste testing after a week of fermentation and move on to the next step once you are happy with the taste.

If you'd like to flavor your kombucha, split it into smaller glass jars or bottles, and add your favorite flavors, such as 1 inch (2.5 cm) of fresh ginger, a few leaves of fresh mint, a few fresh berries or pieces of other fruits. For a stronger taste, let it ferment for an additional day after flavoring and then store in the fridge.

KIMCHI

The pungent, fermented cabbage with a hot kick is an addictive Korean treat. The recipe here is plant-based and on the simpler side compared to the traditional varieties, but it is no less mouthwatering. Use it as a side or a condiment in sandwiches, or even in sushi, as I came to enjoy it. It is already tasty when fresh, but the flavor develops further as it matures and you get to enjoy the probiotic benefits.

Makes 1 quart (1 L)

Vegetables

1 head Chinese (napa) cabbage

¼ cup (72 g) sea salt

1 baby daikon radish, julienne cut

6 green onions, roughly chopped, green and white parts separated

1 small carrot, chopped

Seasoning

2 tbsp (30 ml) coconut aminos

¼ cup (60 ml) pineapple juice

5 to 6 cloves garlic, chopped

3 tbsp (18 g) peeled and chopped fresh ginger

¼ tsp Korean red pepper powder (gochukaru) or red pepper flakes

2 tbsp (8 g) coconut sugar

1 tbsp (15 ml) chickpea miso

As with any fermented foods, make sure you are using a clean surface and utensils for making kimchi. Rinse the cabbage, cut it in half lengthwise and then slice each half crosswise into 2-inch (5-cm) pieces. Discard the hard root part. Place the cabbage in a large bowl and sprinkle with the salt. Toss the cabbage until coated with the salt. Fill the bowl with cold water until all the cabbage pieces are fully submerged. Cover the bowl and let it rest overnight.

In a food processor, combine all the seasoning ingredients with ¼ cup (60 ml) of warm water and process into a paste Drain the cabbage and squeeze out as much excess water as you can with clean hands. Add all the vegetables and the seasoning mixture to the cabbage. Put on rubber gloves (to avoid irritating your skin due to the hot pepper) and massage the vegetables with the seasoning mixture until they are all thoroughly coated.

You will need a quart-size (1-L) glass jar with an airtight lid. Sanitize both the jar and the lid with boiling water. Transfer the kimchi mixture to the jar, press down firmly and tightly close the lid. Let the sealed jar sit in a cool, dark place for 24 hours, and then chill the jar in the fridge for another 3 to 4 days. It will keep in the fridge for up to a month.

FAST PICKLED CUCUMBERS

Pickled cucumber is one of the most favorite condiments of all time. While it is readily sold everywhere, its probiotic properties are best realized with a homemade version. This quick recipe is a great start.

Makes 1 quart (946 ml)

3 tbsp (45 ml) cider vinegar

1½ tbsp (38 g) kosher or pickling salt

½ tsp crushed red pepper flakes

2 tsp (3 g) black peppercorns

2 cloves garlic, peeled

3 large sprigs fresh dill

1 bay leaf

1 large cucumber, sliced

Prepare the pickling brine in a large bowl by combining 1½ cups (355 ml) of water, the vinegar and the salt and mix well. Place the remaining ingredients, except the cucumbers, in a quart-size (1-L) glass jar with an airtight lid. Cut off and discard the ends of the cucumber, slice and pack into the jar. Add the pickling brine and top with additional water, if needed, until the jar is filled to within ½ inch (2.5 cm) from the top. Close the lid and shake well. Store in the fridge for 2 days without opening the jar. Open after 2 days and consume within a week after opening.

BEET KVASS WITH GINGER

When fermented, beets lose most of their sweetness, giving way to an earthy, sour and salty taste that is a delightful addition to salads, sauces and sandwiches. The juice itself can be enjoyed as a cleansing tonic. You get the strong antioxidant benefits of the beets and the superpowers of ginger along with probiotic properties.

Makes 1 quart (1 L)

2 beets, roughly chopped

1 tbsp (6 g) chopped fresh ginger

2 tsp (12 g) unrefined sea salt or Himalayan salt

2¾ cups (650 ml) filtered or spring water

Sanitize a 1-quart (1-L) jar with boiling water; do this near or in the sink to avoid burning yourself. Place the beets, ginger and salt in the jar, add the filtered water and mix until the salt dissolves. Close the jar lid tightly and store in a dark, cool place to ferment for 2 weeks. When it is ready, strain the beets and pour the liquid into another clean jar, close the lid and store in the fridge for up to a month. The next time you make the kvass, you can replace ¼ cup (60 ml) of the water with the kvass liquid you already have saved as a starter. It will be ready in a few days instead of weeks.

ACKNOWLEDGMENTS

So many heartfelt thanks to everyone who ever tasted my food and tried my recipes, to anyone who ever provided me feedback personally or through social media, to all my Instagram peeps who never fail to provide my daily dose of inspiration. I love you all. This book is as much born through the endless support and encouragement of my husband, Emre, and my son, Kevin, as it was through my efforts; they made for wonderful test subjects, too. I am also lucky to be working with Page Street Publishing, and thankful to everyone there, particularly Marissa Giambelluca, who were patient enough to guide me and aid me through every step of the publication process.

ABOUT THE AUTHOR

MAYA SOZER is a culinary creative and a photographer who is passionate about contributing to the growth of the plant-based cuisine. A former professional chef, she draws inspiration from her Mediterranean roots as well as the world cuisine, often fusing the two. Her recipes are guided by her longtime commitment to healthy and practical home cooking. She is the creator of the Dreamy Leaf blog and the author of the cookbook *Easy Vegan Breakfasts & Lunches*. She now lives in Charlotte, North Carolina, with her family, and when she is not cooking, she loves practicing yoga, calisthenics and being outdoors.

INDEX